Organic Gardening for Beginners

How To Grow A Healthy Organic Garden, Naturally: All You Need To Know For A Bountiful Harvest!

G.F. Quinn

Quinn Publishing

Copyright © 2024 by G.F. Quinn

All rights reserved.

No portion of this book may be reproduced in any form without written permission from the publisher or author, except as permitted by U.S. copyright law.

This publication is designed to provide accurate and authoritative information in regard to the subject matter covered. It is sold with the understanding that neither the author nor the publisher is engaged in rendering legal, investment, accounting or other professional services. While the publisher and author have used their best efforts in preparing this book, they make no representations or warranties with respect to the accuracy or completeness of the contents of this book and specifically disclaim any implied warranties of merchantability or fitness for a particular purpose. No warranty may be created or extended by sales representatives or written sales materials. The advice and strategies contained herein may not be suitable for your situation. You should consult with a professional when appropriate. Neither the publisher nor the author shall be liable for any loss of profit or any other commercial damages, including but not limited to special, incidental, consequential, personal, or other damages.

Book Cover by Mehreen Shaukat

Year of Publication: 2024

Contents

1. Introduction — 1
2. USDA Hardiness Zones — 6
3. Organic Gardening — 16
4. Organic Soil Preparation — 38
5. Growing A Naturally Healthy Organic Garden — 57
6. Making Use of Natural Resources — 78
7. Composting and Recycling Used Trash — 92
8. The Organic Solution to Weed and Pest Control — 101
9. How to Harvest, Store, and Winterize an Organic Garden. — 138
10. Conclusion — 158
11. Thank You From the Author — 160
12. Resources — 162
13. Also by G.F. Quinn — 164

Chapter 1
Introduction

Thank you for choosing "Organic Gardening for Beginners." When asked why I write about gardening, it has been a passion of mine for many, many years. Ever since I was a kid, I have been asking my mother questions. Over the years, I have met many amazing people with the same passion for gardening, and their popularity has really grown in the last few years.

Many beginner gardeners might find all the information I provide in this book about gardening a bit overwhelming, especially when it comes to the basics of organic gardening or general gardening knowledge. I consider myself very blessed to have that knowledge passed down to me, which I will share with all of you. In my early days of gardening, I was a bit frustrated as it didn't always go the way I wanted it to. Sure, I had my mom, whom I could lean on for more accurate information, tips she learned over the years from her mom, and so on.

Another narrative is that people believe that gardening is backbreaking work. Sure, it is very enjoyable, but as I have learned over the years, try and make it simple: everyone should love gardening. I have put forth this book with my love for gardening, all while changing that old belief that gardening is extremely difficult.

Having your very own organic garden is also an excellent way to create nutritious foods for yourself and your loved ones. When you buy vegetables from the supermarket, it's not the same as serving a salad to your family that came entirely from your garden and was made with your own two hands.

Many people opt to garden so that they can manage the type of food they eat without worrying about chemicals or preservatives. Commercially grown vegetables are frequently grown in greenhouses and treated with pesticides and chemicals to promote growth.

A quick review of these artificial applications can be unsettling for anyone. Chemical pesticides have serious adverse effects on the human body. Many people are getting on the "organic bandwagon" to reduce the risks to themselves and their loved ones that are frequently associated with commercially produced foods. You do not have to be a health nut to enjoy organic gardening. Imagine how great it will feel to serve foods that were grown naturally, without the risks associated with the use of chemical fertilizers and pesticides.

Many people, including me, are thrilled to see their first red, ripe tomato or stalk of corn emerge from the ground. Organic gardening is also a fantastic way to provide healthy foods for yourself and your family. Buying veggies at the store is not the same as making a salad from your own garden for your family. However, before you begin or intend to cultivate an organic garden, ask yourself the following questions:

- **Do I have to grow it?** One example is corn. Can I grow it? I surely can. However, it can take up a lot of space and produce low yields per square foot.

- **Will it thrive in my garden?.** This is an extremely crucial question that is sometimes missed. Crops have varied requirements. It makes little sense to waste valuable growing space on a crop that will not flourish, mature, or produce in your environment or location.

- **Will it save me money?** In my limited space, I like to grow high-value crops such as heirloom tomatoes, eggplants, and peppers. An heirloom tomato can cost up to $5 per pound at the market. Growing my own is both cost-effective and satisfying.

- **Do I actually like it?** We've all fallen into the trap of cultivating something that doesn't turn out to taste as good as we hoped. One example is celery. Homegrown celery, in my experience, does not taste like what we are used to.

- **Can I preserve it?** Harvest preservation is an essential component of your overall self-sufficiency and gardening strategy. Growing organic foods that can easily be dehydrated, canned, frozen, pickled, or fermented and processed in a variety of ways will greatly assist you in being more self-sufficient.

- **How versatile is it?** Variety is the spice of life. Growing organic crops that can be converted into a variety of cuisines will keep you involved and interested.

Many gardeners look to seed catalogs for inspiration. With so many colors, textures, and variations to choose from, it's easy to become overwhelmed. My method is slightly different. I get inspiration from cookbooks, restaurants, and my favorite chefs. I look at what they're doing, what speaks to me, and what's innovative and compelling. I determine what I want to preserve and enjoy in the winter. I reflect on what I want to share with my friends, family, and community. A lot goes into the planning process, and I encourage you to read my book:

Type 2 Diabetes Cookbook for Beginners: Quick and Easy Mouth-Watering Recipes to Help Manage Type 2 Diabetes: A Better Way to Eat Healthy Without Sacrificing Your Taste Buds!

Enjoy some of my favorite in-depth recipes for living a healthier lifestyle!

That being said, for many people, it is unclear what "organic gardening" looks like or implies. The phrase "organic" is commonly used on product labels and in the media, but what exactly does it mean? Quite simply, organic gardening is all about growing plants without using synthetic chemicals or genetically modified organisms (GMOs). This means that no chemical pesticides, insecticides, herbicides, fertilizers, or GMOs are utilized.

Instead of artificial inputs, organic gardens rely on natural elements such as composting, mulching, and beneficial insects to keep the soil healthy and pest-free. This method of gardening works with nature rather than against it. When you see a food item labeled "organic" at the grocery store, it signifies it was grown or manufactured without the use of synthetic chemicals or genetically modified ingredients. This label does not necessarily imply that the item was cultivated in an organic garden; rather, it indicates that specific requirements have been met during the production or growing process.

In other words, something might be classified as "organic" even if it was not cultivated in an organic garden. Something grown in an organic garden, on the other hand, will always meet the requirements for the designation "organic." When you really think about it, organic gardening is actually quite simple and has been called the easiest of all gardening, all while being the most cost-effective.

Truth be told, it is one of my favorite ways to garden. Because you are outside in nature, gardening organically teaches you to be one with the outside world and how to grow a successful, healthy organic garden. By learning to work with nature, you will rapidly discover that it already does the majority of the work for you via its complex systems. If you are migrating from standard gardening methods to organic gardening methods, you will find that, after learning the fundamentals of organic gardening, you will no longer engage in certain practices.

This transformation will also help you become more aware of everything you do in and around your garden and how your activities affect everything around you. Unfortunately, no one is born with a green thumb; rather, gardening is a very useful talent that can be developed through nothing more than hands-on experience. This will inevitably result in failures, but they should not be taken too seriously, as this is your opportunity to be the gardener you know you can become."Organic gardening for beginners" is designed to be a quick reference resource for new or inexperienced gardeners.

Learning these fundamentals can help you build a solid foundation for all of your gardening endeavors. As you progress in your gardening activities, use this book as a reference to help you establish the foundation of information needed to improve your gardening skills year after year.

Let us begin our journey with "Organic Gardening for Beginners"!

Chapter 2

USDA Hardiness Zones

What Are They?

A rnold Arboretum created the USDA plant hardiness map in 1927 after analyzing plants' ability to live in various climatic situations.

Almost a century later, the United States Department of Agriculture maintains this map, which is regarded as a valuable resource for assisting people not only in the United States but all over the world in determining which plants are suitable for growth in their geographic area and climatic conditions.

So, given its humble beginnings nearly a century ago, what information does the USDA Hardiness Zones map provide, and how can it be used to help us with our gardening practices?

When it comes to gardening, the USDA Plant Hardiness Zones are commonly brought up. The map has been divided into thirteen zones. Gardeners can use the map to determine which perennial plants will grow in their specific climate zone and which will not survive the coldest winter temperatures on average.

Each of the thirteen zones is divided into ten Fahrenheit parts and five Fahrenheit half sections. This map depicts the average of temperature data collected over ten years. It is interesting to note that this map is refreshed every ten years. In reality, the zones traveled northward at a rate of 131 miles per decade.

Before making a purchase, consult the USDA Hardiness Zone chart to determine which perennials flourish in your area. Since this map was last updated in 2023,

Please keep in mind that the USDA Hardiness zones are only basic guidelines. Your specific area may differ for a number of reasons. As a result, I recommend using one of the accessible online tools to match your residence zip code to a hardiness zone.

Please visit the USDA website https://planthardiness.ars.usda.gov/ on a frequent basis to see whether your growth zone has changed. Several hardiness zones turned northward.

In Canada, visit the website: http://planthardiness.gc.ca/?m=1

In the United Kingdom, visit the website: https://www.gardenia.net/guide/hardiness-zones-in-the-united-kingdom

Drawbacks of the hardiness zones map

The hardiness zone map should not be used only to determine which vegetables to grow. It only shows the minimal temperatures in a certain area and the plants that can survive at those temperatures.

It does not account for other elements that influence growth patterns, including humidity, elevation, and frost dates.

As a result, the hardiness map alone will not clearly indicate whether individual plants may survive in a given zone. Supplemental information should be used to help you learn as much as possible about the location and the factors that may influence weather patterns and climate.

An example of how hardiness zones may provide insufficient information may be found in the Western Region of the United States, where the hardiness zone map does not provide a clear indicator of local temperature conditions because to the large fluctuation across places that are closely connected.

In such cases, it is advisable to enhance the information with sunset climate zones. The map also does not indicate freeze dates, precipitation, or elevation, all of which are important considerations when planning garden requirements.

The USDA Hardiness Zone, on the other hand, indicates specific geographic areas and the temperatures found there, as well as suggested plants that will grow in the specified location.

You can use this map to generate a list of recommended plants to grow in your area. With this plant list in hand, you can look at a region's frost dates to determine when the optimum time to plant the listed plants is.

Knowledge of the area's precipitation and elevation in relation to the needs of the plants that can grow there will result in a better understanding of which plants you will be able to cultivate successfully.

World hardiness zones

The use of hardiness zones has extended over the world, as indicated by an increase in their representation from the originally specified 11 USDA hardiness zones to the currently available 13 hardiness zones.

The map has become a standard that is used in many locations to help people comprehend the temperature conditions in their area.

Creating localized versions of the hardiness map has proven to be an effective tool for helping local farmers organize their gardening efforts. Africa, Australia, Canada, China, Japan, New Zealand, Russia, and other regions have developed their own hardiness zone charts.

A cursory look at the global hardiness zone maps reveals that they are consistent with the regional climatic variables that we described before. As a result, Mediterranean climates are often suitable for agriculture, regardless of location.

The USDA Hardiness Zone Map, when combined with other resources such as frost dates and sunset climatic zones, allows you to suggest not only which plants to grow in different places but also the optimal times for planting.

Frost dates

Frost dates is another term you'll hear frequently. Especially the date of your last spring frost. (often when gardeners begin planting outside) and the date of your first fall frost.

There are several reasons why these two dates are important, and you will probably use them repeatedly. It's best to get to know them right away.

In fact, these dates correspond to your annuals. Our annual plants are insufficiently hardy to withstand our harsh winters.

Check the date of your most recent spring frost to determine whether it is safe to plant frost-sensitive plants outdoors on the ground.

This date can help you determine when to start indoor seedlings in preparation for the final spring frost. This is to ensure that they are mature enough to endure the elements outside.

The date of your first fall frost is equally significant. This date indicates how much time you have left to plant certain plants during your entire growing season.

This ensures that before the cold kills the plant, you can harvest something. The time between these two dates is also calculated with these two dates.

This computation returns the total number of days in the growth season. Knowing this knowledge is essential for planning a spring, summer, and fall garden in order to maximize your growth season.

The number of days in your growing season will help you decide whether you have enough time to seed some crops outside or if you need to start some plants indoors early in preparation for your last spring frost to lengthen your growing season.

Planning your garden will be easier if you understand your growing season and the average frost dates. Certain crops may only be able to grow during specific seasons. Knowing how long the spring, summer, and fall growing seasons are will benefit you.

Make a sun map

Knowing where the sun and shadows fall in your garden at different times of day will help you determine which plants will thrive in each area.

Making a sun map will guarantee that your plants receive the sunlight they require to grow. Sun mapping is simply drawing a map of where the sun shines and shadows fall in your yard.

You can learn how many hours of sunlight each spot receives and which sections are shaded during the day.

This allows you to plan where to position each type of plant so that they receive enough sunlight while still providing some shade if necessary.

The best time to make your sun map is in the summer, when the days are longer and there is more direct sunshine. Determine which way your garden faces—north, south, east, or west.

Then, using a compass, decide which way is north and draw an arrow pointing northward (it does not have to be precise).

Next, measure and mark the length of each side of your garden on the paper or canvas that represents the space. You should also identify any trees or structures that cast shadows on your landscape.

With this knowledge, you can start drawing out the patterns that light takes through your garden at various times of the day. When planting new plants, use it as a guide to ensure that they receive enough sunlight while avoiding too much shade.

Microclimates

Although you reside in a climate-specific zone, you will notice that your garden has a variety of microclimates generated by natural elements such as shadows, wind, and elevation.

In this way, your garden represents a microcosm of a larger geographic region that is similarly influenced by these factors.

Furthermore, the existence of a tiny pond, a boulder, or even a brick wall can affect your garden's circumstances.

Knowing and understanding the microclimates in your garden can help you choose the ideal location that represents the climatic conditions required for specific plants to thrive.

As a result, in addition to knowing which plants grow in your area, a thorough study of your garden will enable you to place a plant in the most favorable site for growth.

For example, rocks, walls, and sidewalks absorb solar heat. They continue to emit heat even after the sun has set, making them ideal for planting warm plants near them.

On a larger scale than your garden, you will notice that your suburb or city reacts to man-made construction.

The sun is absorbed in your garden by rocks and walls, just as it is absorbed by buildings within city limits.

As a result, metropolitan temperatures are frequently greater than those on the outskirts.

Keep this in mind while designing your garden, as your home's location within the city boundaries or in the open suburbs will affect the general climate of your garden.

When it comes to the sunlight, the time of day when it shines in a given place might have an impact on the vegetation.

For example, the morning sun received from the east is significantly milder than the afternoon sunlight obtained from the west. In the northern hemisphere, any south-facing walls will receive full sun all day, unless shadows obscure them.

As a result, you must be mindful of your home's position as well as the direction your garden faces.

Whether your plants are exposed to the sun in the morning or in the afternoon can have a tremendous impact on their capacity to thrive because different plants have varied requirements in terms of sunlight exposure.

Especially in terms of duration and intensity, which can be influenced by the garden's orientation.

Trees and buildings' shadows diminish the quantity of sunlight and warmth that a garden location receives. You can also lower the temperature in a garden by using compost mulch instead of rock mulch.

It will enhance the number of plants in the region, although rock mulch will keep heat in longer, which you may want to avoid in arid climates.

Low-lying sections of your garden will be colder and hold more moisture than upland areas, which will be warmer and drier.

This knowledge can help you decide which plants to put in these regions, since plants that require less moisture can be grown in drier, elevated areas, and plants that require more moisture should be planted in areas that suit them.

Wind dries up the soil even more, so attempt to make a windbreak by growing tall hedges. However, keep in mind that shrubs cast shadows, which lower temperatures.

Depending on your needs, this could be viewed as a benefit or a challenge. As a result, you must carefully plan your garden in order to understand the impact of each addition on the overall microclimate.

Dry soil can also be caused by the type of soil utilized in your garden. Sandy soils, for example, will dry up faster than clay soils, which retain more water.

As a result, be aware of the soil types in your garden and, if necessary, amend the soil to meet your individual gardening requirements.

Take the time to establish your region's climate, and then learn about the microclimates in your garden and why they exist.

It will allow you to arrange your garden so that you can take advantage of the present climate without having to make several changes to accommodate your plants.

Instead, you can choose plants that are appropriate for your environment and take little upkeep while offering the benefits you desire.

Once you've gone through your garden to determine the components that influence the microclimate, take the time to note your climate in the space below for future reference.

My climate is: _____

My hardiness zone is: _____

Identifying your climate is the first step toward your gardening success.

Chapter 3
Organic Gardening
What is it?

As previously mentioned, organic gardening is the practice of producing plants without using synthetic fertilizers or pesticides. Instead, it uses natural resources like compost and mulch to enrich the soil and deter pests.

Before we get into the details of how to do this, I believe it would be helpful to first discuss the history of organic gardening, what goes into it, modern alternatives to organic farming, and, of course, the numerous benefits of organic gardening.

It all begins with organic matter

The most significant aspect of organic gardening is the organic materials that are used in it. This includes compost, manure, leaves, grass clippings, and other plant-based items. All of these elements are utilized to enrich the soil and provide a healthy living environment for your plants.

Organic matter serves to build up necessary nutrients in the soil, which helps your plants stay healthy and strong. These materials can also aid in retaining moisture in the soil, which is necessary for keeping your plants hydrated.

Let's take a closer look at how we got there and where organic gardening came from.

Organic gardening history

Have you ever wondered why organic gardening has grown so popular in recent years? While the idea of producing plants without the use of artificial fertilizers and pesticides may appear to be a recent phenomenon, organic gardening has its origins in ancient times. It's not a new concept.

Organic farming dates back to ancient times, when farmers utilized manure and other natural fertilizers to help their crops flourish. It was not a trend; it was simply how things were done.

The ancient Egyptians were among the first to understand the benefits of natural fertilizers for their crops. Native American tribes used companion planting to ensure that their gardens had access to all of the nutrients required for growth.

Industrial agriculture, which used chemical fertilizers and pesticides to improve food production, first emerged in the nineteenth century. This increased yields, but it also produced environmental damage in the form of soil erosion and river pollution from chemical runoff.

As people became more aware of the negative consequences, there was a greater demand for more sustainable farming practices.

Sir Albert Howard (1873-1947), an English agricultural scientist who supervised agricultural research facilities in India from 1905 to 1931 before permanently relocating to England, pioneered this concept.

His years of agricultural research and observations led to the development of an organic farming philosophy and concept, which he advocated in various writings, notably An Agricultural Testament (1943).

Howard's approach to soil fertility relied on increasing soil humus with a focus on composting, which he considered critical for preserving soil fertility.

He also pushed for the efficient recycling of waste materials onto farms, such as sewage sludge, which was supported by F.H. King's book Farmers of Forty Centuries (1911). Howard invented a composting technology that was subsequently extensively utilized.

Lord Northbourne created the term "organic farming" in the 1940s, and he helped promote it among farmers. Later, J.I. Rodale published "The Organic Gardening and Farming Guide," which detailed his vision for an agricultural system devoid of chemical fertilizers and pesticides.

This book sparked an organic farming movement that is still going strong today, with many farmers abandoning industrial agriculture in favor of more sustainable methods including crop rotation, composting, and intercropping.

Today, the Rodale Institute continues its work through educational programs and scientific research projects on organic food systems.

Organic and non-organic gardening, according to Rodale and Howard, were two opposing agricultural concepts. For many years, organic and nonorganic farming competed, with organic agriculture only gaining significant traction in the 1980s when the USDA issued recommendations for organic farming.

Later, the passage of the Federal Organic Food Production Act in the 1990s began to pave the way for commercial organic farming in the United States.

In today's world, organic gardening is a hugely popular movement, with millions of individuals throughout the world preferring to grow their own food without using artificial fertilizers or pesticides.

From ancient times to the present, farmers have embraced organic practices to produce high-quality food while simultaneously safeguarding our environment for future generations. And this is unlikely to change in the near future.

What really takes place in organic gardening?

Organic gardening focuses on using natural materials and methods to grow healthy plants. Sure. But how? Let us take a closer look at how you can create your own natural garden.

Avoid using pesticides, herbicides, or synthetic chemicals

The most crucial aspect of organic gardening is avoiding chemicals. This type of gardening simply involves growing plants without using chemical pesticides or fertilizers.

It involves using natural approaches like companion planting, crop rotation, composting, and mulching rather than chemical-based ones.

Composting

Composting is an important aspect of organic gardening since it promotes better, more sustainable soil for your plants.

It is the process of combining organic materials like leaves, grass clippings, kitchen scraps, and animal manure and breaking them down by bacteria and other organisms to create a nutrient-rich soil supplement called compost.

The goal of composting is to provide critical nutrients that may be used to help plants grow faster and stronger.

It could also improve soil quality by introducing helpful microbes, breaking up hard soils, retaining moisture, and delivering critical minerals like nitrogen, phosphorus, and potassium that are required for healthy plant growth.

Additionally, compost can help minimize the quantity of water required in the garden by retaining moisture in the soil.

Composting also helps to minimize waste by encouraging the recycling of food scraps and other materials that might otherwise wind up in landfills or incinerators.

Finally, compost reduces pollutants from fertilizer runoff by acting as a natural fertilizer.

There is also compost tea. Compost tea is prepared by infusing water with compost material and steeping it like tea before applying it to your plants. Compost tea aids in disease prevention, root growth, plant nourishment, and more!

It's also ideal for supplementing nutrients in between normal fertilizer treatments or when new plants require immediate feeding.

Companion planting

Companion planting, an age-old method in which different types of plants are combined to enhance their respective benefits, is an important aspect of organic gardening.

Simply explained, companion planting is the technique of carefully arranging specific plants next to one another to promote the overall health of your garden.

Various plants have varied impacts on one another, which might be useful or damaging, depending on the combination you choose.

For example, some plants may repel dangerous insects, while others attract beneficial pollinators. By carefully selecting which plants to place in your garden, you may optimize their individual benefits while reducing any potential conflicts with one another.

One of the most significant benefits of companion planting is that it reduces pests in your garden without using harsh chemicals or pesticides.

Certain plant combinations can naturally repel harmful insects while attracting helpful ones, such as pollinators or ladybugs, which feed on pests without harming your crops.

This means you don't have to worry about using harsh chemicals or costly pest control services to keep your garden safe from pests.

Plus, companion planting can help increase the overall health and productivity of your garden by providing additional nutrients to particular plants and helping them grow better than they would if they were planted alone.

And let's not forget another important benefit: shade. Companion planting can provide natural shade for certain crops while letting sunlight into others, allowing you to achieve a greater yield from each plant in your garden.

Cover cropping

Cover cropping is an important aspect of organic gardening since it allows gardeners to preserve healthy soil while also increasing crop output.

Cover cropping is the technique of planting one or more crops between rows of vegetables to protect the soil from erosion when the vegetable crop is not growing.

This crop can be produced on either shallow or tilled soil, but it must be planted before the main vegetable crop is sown.

Cover crops are often planted in late summer or early spring and then tilled into the soil before new planting begins in late spring or early summer.

One of the most significant advantages of cover cropping is that it protects soils from erosion caused by wind and water runoff. Cover crops also add valuable nutrients to your soil, such as nitrogen and phosphate, increasing its production over time.

They can serve as a type of pest control by attracting beneficial insects that eat destructive bugs. Cover crops also help to control weed development by competing for resources such as sunlight and water.

Mulch

Mulch is any material used to cover the soil's surface in order to prevent erosion, preserve moisture, minimize weed development, and improve soil fertility.

Mulch can be made from a variety of materials, including wood chips, bark chips, straws, grass clippings, shredded leaves, pine needles, gravel, and newspaper.

Mulch helps to maintain a healthy organic garden by minimizing water loss through evaporation and regulating soil temperature.

During hot summer days, when temperatures exceed 90 degrees Fahrenheit for more than five days in a row, mulch keeps your plants cool by providing shade over their roots and preventing water loss from occurring too quickly.

Mulch also helps to inhibit weeds, which can be difficult to control without the use of chemical herbicides or other synthetic items. Covering the dirt with mulch prevents weed seeds from sprouting and maturing into adult plants.

Furthermore, mulch improves soil quality by providing organic matter, which offers critical nutrients to your plants while also increasing water retention capacity. It also stimulates microbial activity in the soil, which converts organic matter into plant-available nutrients.

Whenever Possible, use Native Plants and Avoid Using GMOs

Using native plants whenever possible and avoiding genetically modified organisms (GMOs) are both important aspects of organic gardening.

Native plants are simply those that grow naturally in an area. They've adapted to the region's climate, soil, and conditions, making them more likely to thrive than non-native plants.

By selecting native plants for your garden, you can save time on care and upkeep because they do not require any adjustments or modifications to adapt to the natural habitat. This also helps to conserve resources such as water, as most native plants require little additional irrigation.

Genetically modified organisms (GMOs) are plants that have been altered in a laboratory setting to produce something new, such as faster-growing crops or crops that are resistant to pests or extreme weather conditions.

While these changes may appear advantageous on paper, they might pose issues in nature because these new inventions do not normally occur in the ecosystem.

More research is needed to evaluate whether GMSO foods are eventually safe for human consumption. For these reasons, it is generally recommended to avoid GMOs wherever possible.

By utilizing native plants and avoiding GMOs, you may contribute to sustainable practices while still enjoying a lovely garden with rich greenery.

Your garden will not only be visually appealing, but it will also contribute to biodiversity by providing a habitat for local wildlife such as birds and butterflies.

Furthermore, if you choose to harvest any vegetables from your garden, you can be confident that whatever you consume is natural and free of any potential hazards linked to GMOs.

Alternative methods to organic gardening

Now that you've learned about organic gardening, what are the alternatives?

The most obvious example is the use of synthetic products in the garden, such as chemical fertilizer and herbicides.

These have certain advantages: they are more immediately absorbed and utilized by plants, unlike fertilizers, which means you don't have to wait months or years to see your fertility improve.

Chemicals are also extremely effective at pest control, killing them quickly, so you may go about your gardening.

However, they are not the only tactics employed in modern agriculture (the "non" organic side of things).

Monocrop planting is a popular trend in today's agriculture. Monocrop planting occurs when only one type of crop is planted in a field or garden.

This approach has various advantages, including increased harvest efficiency and improved yield predictability.

However, monocropping can make soil prone to erosion and nutrient depletion; therefore, crop rotation and replenishment with compost or other natural ingredients are essential.

Growing only one crop may be more profitable for commercial farmers in some situations, but it has little use in the backyard garden.

Tilling is another type of practice. Tilling is the process of turning over soil to aerate it and get it ready for planting. It helps to break up huge dirt clumps, allowing water and air to infiltrate the soil more quickly.

Tilling also stimulates microbial activity, which assists plant growth; however, too much tilling can deplete the soil of nutrients and, if done incorrectly, can lead to compacted soil.

Tilling is not always a nonorganic method, but it can be harmful if used as the sole method of promoting soil aeration.

Organic gardeners may try no-till farming methods, which rely on careful crop selection and spacing rather than tilling, for improved results.

A final nonorganic technique is to develop hybrid and non-GMO crops. Hybrid plants are developed by crossing two different species of plants to produce offspring with desired features from both parents (for example, disease resistance).

Again, GMO crops are those that scientists have genetically manipulated to obtain desirable traits (such as drought resistance).

While these methods may result in higher yields or better resistance to pests or weather conditions, there are also possible downsides, such as decreased biodiversity due to a lack of genetic variation among crops generated through engineering or hybridization.

With that in mind, let's examine the many benefits of organic gardening as a viable option.

Beneficial to the environment

Organic gardening is a vital approach for all of us to help conserve our planet while also enjoying all of its natural beauty. Let us take a deeper look at its numerous benefits.

Adding organic matter to the soil

Compost, leaf mold, wood chips, and manure can all be used to enrich the soil in an organic garden. This improves its structural integrity and ability to retain moisture and nutrients.

Adding organic matter also boosts the activity of microbes, which help break down organic material into nutrients that plants can consume.

It also supplies food for helpful insects like earthworms, which aerate and fertilize the soil. This reduces the need for chemical fertilizers, which can harm groundwater supplies.

There are fewer chemicals in the soil

Organic gardens use natural methods rather than chemicals to repel pests and nourish plants.

Companion planting (growing two species of plants near each other) is a natural pest control approach that can repel certain pests or attract helpful insects like ladybugs, which feed on aphids and mites that would otherwise harm plants.

Natural fertilizers like compost and manure produce nutrient-rich soil without introducing hazardous chemicals into the ecosystem.

Protects beneficial insects

Beneficial insects such as bees and ladybugs thrive in organic gardens, pollinating flowers and naturally keeping pests away from crops.

Avoiding chemical pesticides creates a more conducive atmosphere for these beneficial creatures, ensuring that your garden is full of life.

Protects soil microbes

The use of synthetic fertilizers in conventional farming kills soil bacteria that are necessary for optimal plant growth.

Organic gardening helps to minimize this destruction by avoiding chemical fertilizers entirely and instead depending on natural resources such as compost or manure for nourishment, thereby maintaining vital microorganisms in the soil required for good plant growth!

Ensures long-term soil health

Organic gardening promotes healthy soil by employing natural fertilizers like compost or manure, which are high in nutrients and help support healthy soil bacteria and fungi.

This means that plants have access to nutrients while naturally preserving soil structure and reducing erosion.

Maintains the health of river systems

Using synthetic chemical fertilizers can cause runoff into streams, rivers, and ponds. Organic farming eliminates this risk because no pollutants are used during the process.

Natural materials, such as compost, degrade slowly and gradually release nutrients into the surrounding environment, posing no harm to adjacent water sources or wildlife habitats.

Furthermore, organic materials absorb more carbon dioxide from the atmosphere than synthetic fertilizers, helping to reduce overall greenhouse gas emissions.

Enhances the natural environment of several species

Many animal species, including birds, insects, small mammals, reptiles, and amphibians, live in organic gardens and rely on plants for food and shelter.

By providing them with a safe sanctuary free of pesticides and other pollutants, you can ensure that your garden is a perfect habitat for these critters, who would otherwise struggle due to habitat degradation or urban growth.

Furthermore, it provides pollinators, such as bees, with locations to forage securely without coming into contact with potentially hazardous compounds employed in traditional farming practices.

Plant disease resistance has improved

Chemical fertilizers and pesticides can harm your plants' natural defenses against disease. This makes them more vulnerable to fungus, mildew, and other illnesses that can devastate your crops.

However, by employing organic approaches such as crop rotation and companion planting, you can improve your plants' disease resistance while avoiding undesirable side effects.

Reduced erosion

Soil erosion is a major concern in modern agriculture. Chemical fertilizers and pesticides can leach into surrounding streams and rivers, contaminating them with harmful compounds.

Organic gardening solves this problem by using natural methods like cover cropping and mulching to protect the soil from water runoff.

As a result, you'll have healthier soil, which means healthier plants and fewer toxins entering local streams.

Financial benefits

Organic gardening is becoming increasingly popular as individuals seek ways to reduce their environmental impact.

Aside from the environmental benefits, producing your own vegetables has multiple financial benefits. Organic food can be pricey, but growing your own produce is one way to offset rising shopping prices.

Even if you don't have much space in your yard, you can produce a variety of vegetables in containers or raised beds. Start small and progressively expand your garden as you become more acquainted with the procedure.

You might be shocked at how much money you can save on groceries just by growing a portion of your own food. When it comes to creating an organic garden, many people believe they must invest in costly tools and supplies.

However, this is not always the case—there are numerous ways to save money on gardening goods. Instead of purchasing costly fertilizers and insecticides, opt for natural alternatives like compost and helpful insects like ladybugs or praying mantises.

Mulch can also be made from fallen leaves, or you can mix your own soil using household products. With a little imagination, you can keep prices low while still producing excellent results from your organic garden.

Finally, growing an organic garden can be a lucrative side hustle. Enterprising gardeners even find methods to make money from their gardens!

If you have excess food after harvesting what you need for yourself, consider selling it at local farmer's markets or joining a community-supported agriculture (CSA) program, which charges a fixed fee for weekly delivery boxes loaded with fresh produce from local farms and gardens.

This is an excellent method for increasing your income while also allowing others to benefit from your efforts!

Other benefits

We know that growing organic is excellent for the environment and natural resources, but did you know there are many more benefits to having your own organic garden?

Improved health

Growing your own organic vegetables ensures that you know exactly what is in your diet. You may be confident that it is free of chemicals, additives, and potentially harmful pesticides and herbicides.

Eating clean, healthy food on a daily basis can have a significant impact on our bodies because these foods contain fewer pollutants, including heavy metals.

You can try other things

With an organic garden, you won't have to deal with "the same old thing" day after day. To add diversity to your diet, try experimenting with different types of plants and vegetables.

This not only keeps things interesting from a culinary standpoint, but it also provides additional possibilities for your body to absorb nutrients.

Better taste

One of the best benefits of having an organic garden is being able to eat fresh fruits and veggies directly from the soil!

When produce is left to ripen on the vine or stalk before being harvested (rather than being selected early for transportation), it develops its full flavor potential, which makes a significant difference in taste.

Plus, because you are not utilizing any harsh chemicals or pesticides while producing organically, your product will have no bad aftertastes or off flavors.

Increased nutritional value

Did you know that many vegetables, grains, and fruits today have fewer vitamins and minerals than those harvested decades ago? That is alarming, but you may be able to solve it if you create your own organic garden.

As previously mentioned, organically cultivated food includes fewer contaminants and higher quantities of vitamins and minerals.

According to studies, produce harvested from an organic garden contains up to 20% more antioxidants than conventional produce, which can help reduce inflammation and prevent disease.

The spiritual value

There is something unique about raising one's own food that cannot be described in words; some would even claim that it is spiritual!

Many people find it extremely peaceful and centering to let nature take its course, from planting seeds to harvesting.

Furthermore, by engaging with nature in this manner, you will gain a greater respect for life itself.

Strengthens local community connections

Organic gardening is a great way to make new friends and enhance current ones. When you raise your own food through organic gardening, you are participating in an activity that not only provides real benefits but is also extremely fulfilling.

You are a part of something bigger than yourself—a common aim to offer nutritious, delicious meals to your community. This common interest fosters an environment in which people are more inclined to bond over their shared passion for organic gardening.

Not only that, but when people garden together, they learn how to collaborate and solve difficulties (for example, pest control).

Working together to achieve a shared goal promotes trust and respect among all project participants. This trust can then be expanded to other activities, such as volunteering or neighborhood watch programs.

In this approach, organic gardening acts as a catalyst for the formation of deep ties between neighbors who might not otherwise interact with one another.

Organic gardening challenges

The urge to live a more self-sufficient lifestyle through organic gardening is growing among individuals who wish to take control of their food supply. However, organic farming is not without its obstacles.

Fortunately, there are solutions to overcome these obstacles and simplify organic gardening.

However, understanding the problems of organic growing is essential before learning how to overcome them—and, eventually, becoming successful with your new backyard garden.

Let us take a quick look at some of these obstacles.

It takes more work

Organic growing involves more work than using synthetic fertilizers or pesticides. This means that your garden will need regular weeding, pruning, and mulching to thrive.

But don't be discouraged! With some forethought and determination, you can keep up with your garden without becoming overwhelmed by the added work.

Carving aside a few hours each week to care for your garden may be a fun hobby with tasty benefits.

And, over time, you'll likely discover that you can design systems that build on one another to create a garden that requires little effort while producing satisfying long-term benefits.

When switching from regular to organic gardening methods, it takes time to see results—sometimes up to two years!

It takes time to enhance soil health and structure to the point where it can support healthy garden growth.

This can be disappointing when all you want is fresh vegetables immediately!

But if you are patient and consistent in caring to your garden, your efforts will eventually pay off in the form of plentiful yields.

Can Occasionally Be Pricey

Organic gardening is frequently associated with expensive expenses because it requires the purchase of resources such as composters or greenhouses.

These may not appear necessary at first glance, and in most situations, all you need for an organic garden is a shovel and some compost (which you can make right on the ground outside—no need for an expensive system).

Organic gardening can be as inexpensive or as expensive as you like, but there is a case to be made for making some initial investments.

Investing in these equipment can save you money in the long term by protecting your plants from hazardous elements and pests, eliminating the need for expensive synthetic chemicals or pesticides.

Requires Knowledge

Finally (and maybe most importantly), gardening organically requires a large amount of knowledge. Acquiring this knowledge can be tough if you are new to organic gardening.

Fortunately, there are other internet resources accessible that provide useful advice, and this book is one of them!

Develop a Plan for Your Organic Garden

It's fun to think about digging into your soil and planting herb and vegetable gardens. Before you get your hands dirty, take note of your growing conditions.

Determine which plants thrive in your area and which vegetables and fruits you wish to raise. Make a list of the plants you want to use to improve the soil, attract helpful insects, or provide organic food for your table.

Begin a garden notebook to record your experiences and inspirations as you go through the following chapters.

Chapter 4

Organic Soil Preparation

As my understanding of organic gardening expanded, so did my enjoyment of working with my plants.

It is real science, and researchers discovered several years ago that certain soil bacteria known as Mycobacterium vaccae might promote serotonin production in the brain.

Serotonin is one of the happy hormones, which boosts mood, sleep, hunger, and memory. (Raypole, 2019).

According to studies, anxiety and depression are connected with low levels of serotonin.

In a mouse test, the researchers discovered that exposure to Mycobacterium vaccae bacteria in soil altered mice's behaviors in the same manner that antidepressants did.

The mice also had higher levels of biochemical markers in their brains, indicating an elevated presence of serotonin (Lowry et al., 2007).

It's no surprise that 49% of people who started organic gardening during the pandemic said it improved their mental health (National Gardening Association, 2021).

If good soil is beneficial to mental health, then it is also necessary for healthy plants.

What exactly does a plant require to grow?

Plants require four basic conditions to thrive:

- Light
- Water
- Air
- Nutrients.

If you can meet those four requirements in an acceptable space, you're well on your way to creating a thriving garden.

It's easy to see how plants obtain light, water, and air, but what nutrients do they require and where do they originate from?

Plants require seventeen key nutrients to flourish. Three of these nutrients, carbon, oxygen, and hydrogen, come from air and water, but the remaining 14 must be taken by the plant's roots through the soil.

Soil that lacks any of these nutrients will limit the plant's growth potential. Plants require some nutrients in greater quantities than others.

Macronutrients are nutrients that must be consumed in large quantities, whereas micronutrients are nutrients that must be consumed in small amounts.

Macronutrients aren't more vital than micronutrients; plants just require more of them.

The six macronutrients required by plants are:

- Nitrogen
- Potassium
- Phosphorus
- Calcium
- Magnesium
- Sulfur

The eight micronutrients required by plants are:

- Chlorine
- Iron
- Boron
- Manganese
- Zinc
- Copper

- Molybdenum
- Nickel

Each nutrient contributes to distinct elements of plant development and health.

Nitrogen, usually known by the chemical abbreviation N, promotes green growth and the formation of stems and leaves.

Phosphorus, or P, promotes photosynthesis and the growth of flowers and fruit.

Potassium, or K, promotes root growth and helps to avoid disease.

A great garden begins with good soil

The soil creates a physical environment in which your plants can develop.

- Good soil has a loose texture that allows roots to flow outward and downward freely. It also has enough structure to support and anchor the plant, preventing it from tipping over on a windy day.
- Good soil holds moisture, does not dry up soon, and provides adequate drainage to keep plants from becoming waterlogged.
- Good soil contains pockets of air between its particles.
- Good soil is high in organic matter.
- Good soil is a biodiverse ecosystem filled with microorganisms,

bacteria, fungi, insects, and worms.

I am thrilled that you have decided to start an organic garden and will use a soil mix. It is essential to have a basic understanding of what soil is and how to keep it healthy.

Soil types

The native soil in your yard will normally be a mixture of the three types listed below, with one being dominant:

- Sand
- Clay
- Silt

Most people are familiar with sandy soil's appearance, which includes visible particles and a gritty texture. It is simple to dig in. When wet, it clumps easily (like a damp sandcastle), yet it also dries quickly (the sandcastle crumbles).

In horticultural terms, it has excellent drainage but poor moisture retention. Sandy soil contains little nutrients; when water rushes swiftly through the particles, nutrients are washed (or leached) away.

Sandy soil is appropriate for producing root crops such as carrots, radishes, and beets, as well as other plants that require good drainage, if nutrient deficiencies are corrected.

Anyone who has tried to dig in native clay understands how tough it can be. When clay soil is wet, it is sticky and dense; when it dries, it can resemble rock.

Clay particles are tiny and consequently closely packed; it has poor drainage and limited accessible air space. It can be nutrient-dense, but because of its other properties, the nutrients may not be readily available for plants to absorb.

Silt-rich soil is thought to be easier to plant in the garden. It has smaller particles than sand but is not as fine as clay. It is quite fertile and holds water effectively.

However, it is easily compacted and resists erosion. Loam soils, which are regarded as the best-growing soils, have an equal amount of sand, clay, and silt.

There are two other types of soil: peat and chalk, which are more common in some regions but less so in North America.

Physical properties of soil

Physical properties determine soil quality.

- Texture,
- Structure
- Pore Space
- Organic Content

Soil texture is determined by the size of its particles. Soils often contain particles ranging in size from vast (such as sand) to so fine that they can only be seen under an electron microscope.

Soils exist on a sliding scale, with sand on one end, clay on the other, and silt in the center. The native soil in your yard will be somewhere in that range.

Structure refers to the ability of soil particles to bind together or form into clumps. Soil that aggregates in various shapes and sizes allows water and air to flow (or infiltrate) via the crevices between the clumps.

Pore spaces are pores that store air and allow water to pass through. The most productive soils have a lot of pore space.

When organic material is introduced into the soil, it behaves like a sponge. It takes water from the pores, allowing plenty of room for air, but then delivers the stored water to the plants when they require it (Spiegel, 2021).

Purchase high-quality soil

Soil is one of the most significant expenditures you can make for your garden; purchasing high-quality soil is important.

When selecting a soil mix for your garden, seek out loose, friable (easy to crumble) soil with a deep color and a rich aroma. Garden centers sell soil in bulk or in bags.

If you're buying bags, read the labels carefully and look for locally sourced materials.

If you buy bulk soil, grab a handful and squeeze it. It should clump together but separate when poked.

Avoid purchasing

- Sticky soil that refuses to break apart; it contains too much clay.
- The soil is light in color.
- Soil with a foul odor.

Many garden centers sell ready-to-buy bulk blends. They are commonly referred to as triple mixes in Canada and 50/50 mixes in the United States.

Both contain a combination of topsoil, compost, and sometimes black loam or peat moss.

Peat moss is currently unpopular among gardeners because it is a non-renewable resource, and harvesting it contributes to global warming.

The amount of soil required for your garden in cubic feet or cubic meters is a straightforward calculation: length x width x height of the frame (if using a raised bed).

An online calculator (Soil Calculator, n.d.) is free to use. Simply search for it online, and you'll be set to go!

Nurturing and maintaining healthy soils

Organic gardening calls for a thorough grasp of the soil, as well as how to nurture and maintain it. Building and keeping healthy soil is a critical component of any successful organic garden.

This means that before planting, you must examine and enhance the structure of your soil, as well as create an ideal atmosphere for plant growth.

The first step toward creating a healthy soil ecosystem is to incorporate nutrients and bulky organic elements like compost.

These components not only provide important nutrients, but they also aid in forming a suitable structure for plant roots to penetrate. There are several soil amendments you can add.

Soil amendments are items used to modify or adjust the physical properties of soil in order to help plants grow more effectively. There are two kinds of amendments: organic and inorganic (mineral).

Organic supplements include compost, manure, seaweed, wood chips or bark mulch, cover crops, green manures, crop residues, peat moss, sawdust, and leaf mold.

These organic additions will progressively increase the soil's organic matter content and beneficial microbes, making nutrients available to plants.

Inorganic (mineral) additions include lime (for acid-loving plants), gypsum (to loosen clay soils), sulfur (to reduce pH levels in alkaline soils), and perlite or vermiculite for aeration.

Inorganic supplements provide rapid benefits to the soil by altering its pH balance or drainage qualities, as opposed to organic amendments, which take time to degrade into plant-usable nutrients.

They also provide a rapid source of minerals like calcium and iron, which may be low in some soils.

Before you plant your garden beds, you should examine your present soil health to discover any deficiencies before adding your desired amendments. However, encouraging soil health does not end with additions.

Other preventive techniques include mulching bare ground and incorporating manure or composted materials into the topsoil layer.

It's also crucial to avoid digging whenever possible because it might disrupt the soil's natural ecosystem, resulting in the loss of beneficial species, lower water retention capacity, and compaction from heavy machinery or cultivation instruments.

Instead of digging up your entire garden bed every season, try no-dig alternatives like planting directly into undisturbed soil or mulching over existing plants.

This will help to maintain a higher diversity of organisms in your soil while also improving moisture retention.

And while planning our plantings, it's critical to make the best use of the nutrients in your garden bed so that plants don't compete for them.

It is also critical to rotate crops so that plants are grown in different parts of your garden each season; this reduces the likelihood of pests and illnesses establishing themselves in any one region of your garden bed as a result of continuous development in the same spot year after year.

Finally, consider growing certain plants, such as green manures, which retain nutrients within their tissues while growing before being returned to the soil; they can also serve as a weed barrier by suppressing them through competition for resources such as light and water.

Encourage biodiversity

One of the most important concepts of organic farming is to promote biodiversity.

What does that mean, and why is it so important?

Biodiversity refers to the variety of life forms found in an ecosystem. It comprises all living creatures, such as plants, animals, fungi, bacteria, and viruses.

A diversified environment with a wide range of species promotes stability because it can better meet the demands of its residents than an ecosystem with a few species.

This is especially true when it comes to pest and disease control or adapting to unexpected environmental changes.

Planting a variety of vegetables, fruits, and flowers helps to minimize the accumulation of soil diseases. You will also provide a range of food sources and habitat for birds and insects.

Encouraging wildlife in our garden will help manage numerous pests. Aphids are eaten by birds and insects, whereas frogs and ground beetles devour slugs.

This means that you will not need to use chemical pesticides because these critters naturally manage the bug population.

Adding well-rotted natural materials, such as handmade compost, will nourish the small soil bacteria and other life forms, including worms.

These soil organisms improve soil structure by digesting waste materials and secreting nutrients that benefit plants.

By creating a diversified environment for these organisms to thrive, you may help ensure that your plants receive the nutrients they require for healthy growth (for a detailed explanation, see Chapter 7).

Don't forget the pollinators. Pollinators are crucial to food production; without them, we would not have anything to eat!

By planting a variety of flowers in your organic garden, you provide an excellent home for pollinators such as bees and butterflies, which require pollen from different plants at different times of the year to thrive.

There are various techniques to increase biodiversity in your organic garden. The first step is to investigate biological pest control methods for any present pest problems you may have.

This could include using predatory insects like ladybugs or praying mantises to control pests without the use of chemicals or pesticides.

Another option to increase biodiversity is to use soil and plant inoculants, such as compost tea or mycorrhizal fungal products, to naturally promote crop development in the absence of chemical fertilizers or soil amendments.

You may also diversify your crop rotation by growing different sorts of plants each season to avoid competition for resources and to attract different types of beneficial insects that will aid in the management of nutrients and pests in your garden.

Use your natural resources responsibly

When feasible, organic growers should utilize natural resources such as wood and plant material. It is preferable to source goods locally to lessen their energy footprint.

Plant-based products are preferred over synthetics since they are biodegradable and renewable.

Compost containers built from hardwood planks or recycled plastic drums are excellent examples of this (for a detailed explanation, see Chapter 6).

If a non-natural resource, such as plastic, is required, consider recycling or reusing it before discarding it at the end of its useful life.

Plastic pots, compost bins, and wheelbarrows are long-lasting enough to be repaired or reused numerous times before they require replacement.

When disposing of used products, always consider recycling rather than putting them in landfills, which degrade the environment with hazardous chemicals and greenhouse gases.

Remember, as an organic grower, you wield purchasing power. You can choose which products to purchase from garden stores and other providers based on whether they use sustainable practices.

Create a nutrient reservoir in the soil

As an organic gardener, one of the most important principles to remember is to create a nutrient reservoir in your soil. This means that instead of using fertilizers, you should concentrate on adding nutrients to your soil that will boost its fertility.

If done correctly, this will result in healthier and more resilient plants and trees, as well as a more sustainable garden.

The first step toward creating a nutrient reservoir in your soil is to conduct fertility control. This means adding components like compost, manure, or mulch to your soil on a regular basis to help it retain nutrients and moisture over time.

By doing this on a regular basis, you can keep your soil healthy and full of helpful bacteria and microbes that will help your plants thrive.

Another method for establishing your "nutrient reservoir" is to use weeds as a sort of reporting device. Weeds are often viewed negatively, as something that must be controlled and eradicated.

However, weeds might indicate whether your soil is good or bad. If there are a lot of weeds growing in our garden beds, it could be due to a high level of nutrients in the soil and a lack of water or aeration.

On the other side, if there are few weeds, it may indicate that the soil lacks the necessary nutrients and minerals required for optimal growth.

Paying attention to weed growth can help you identify what type of fertilizer or amendments are required for optimal health.

In addition to fertility control, utilizing cover crops and green manures is an excellent approach to increasing nutrients in your soil.

Cover crops are plants produced specifically for their ability to replenish organic matter in the soil when they are tilled back in after their life cycle has ended.

Green manures are similar, yet they are frequently utilized when living because their extensive root systems can provide extra benefits, such as weed suppression and erosion prevention.

Both cover crops and green manures can be incredibly efficient at enhancing the condition of your soil over time, with little effort on your side.

Adopt a holistic approach to managing weeds, pests, and diseases

Organic gardening is becoming increasingly popular as more people become aware of the environmental and personal health benefits it may provide.

One of the most important aspects of organic gardening is a holistic approach to weed, insect, and disease management (for a detailed explanation, see Chapter 8).

Weeds are one of the most common issues in every garden, but they do not have to be if you adopt a holistic approach.

Mechanical management techniques such as tilling, hand pulling, mulching, and thermal weed management can help keep weeds under control without the use of chemical herbicides.

Using cover crops or proper spacing between plants can help reduce the number of weeds that sprout up in your garden.

If necessary, you can also use organic herbicides such as vinegar, lemongrass oil, or corn gluten meal, which will help kill existing weeds without harming your soil or plants.

As far as pests and diseases go, it's important to think of the entire garden as a whole rather than individual areas.

Cultural practices such as choosing appropriate varieties for your area, being mindful of where you buy seeds and transplants (to prevent the spread of diseases), planting with companion plants (which can deter pests), crop rotation, and composting can all help prevent pests or diseases from taking hold in your garden.

Using physical methods like diatomaceous earth (or DE) or floating row covers can also protect from pests while still allowing sunlight and water through so that your plants stay healthy.

You might feel inspired to turn to genetically engineered crops for your garden, hoping that the unique traits of these plants will help them better withstand insect and disease pressure.

There are both pros and cons associated with this, but it's important to note that the National Organic Program (NOP) contains rules prohibiting the use of genetically engineered crops or materials derived from such crops in organic gardens.

This means that very few genetically engineered crops are available for home gardeners anyway. So most people don't have to be concerned with organic pest and disease management in their gardens.

Overall, a holistic organic garden concentrates on what it can accept and work with rather than what it must eliminate or destroy.

For example, you may want to leave certain weeds in your garden. Certain weeds, such as dandelions, will not harm crops, but they have deep taproots that can extract nutrients from the soil and promote their growth.

They also benefit pollinators and predatory insects, which help keep destructive ones (such as Japanese beetles) away from your plants.

There are other weeds, like nettles, that provide nutrients for plants and can even be harvested to make plant food.

Insect pests like aphids are food for beneficial insects like hoverflies and ladybirds, and the slug can help feed thrushes and other birds that might be nearby.

If you notice something in your organic garden that shouldn't be there but isn't doing any damage to your plants, your goal should be to work with it rather than try to eliminate it.

This is part of encouraging biodiversity in your garden and building soil, along with fostering a holistic approach to the art of gardening.

Create a healthy, growing environment

The most crucial aspect of organic gardening is to provide an optimal environment for growth. This requires caring for your plants and soil to keep them in top shape throughout their life cycle.

To do this, work with your climate rather than against it by choosing suitable garden sites and using high-quality seeds.

When planning and designing your garden, take into account all environmental factors. Consider the climate in which you reside and choose plants that will thrive there rather than forcing items that may already be doing well in your location.

When determining where to plant each species of plant, consider elements such as sunlight exposure and water availability to maximize development.

To maintain a healthy growth environment, use high-quality seeds and plants, and keep everything clean.

Quality seeds are less likely to have been genetically engineered or treated with toxic chemicals, which can have a long-term negative impact on the health of your garden.

When shopping from internet vendors or garden centers, read customer reviews to ensure you are dealing with credible providers who provide high-quality products.

If feasible, pick up the products instead of having them delivered to ensure their quality before purchasing them.

Wear protective equipment when handling soil or plants, and thoroughly clean instruments after use to avoid accidentally spreading disease from one area of the garden to another.

Be aware that issues frequently originate from failing to detect the first signs of sickness or pest in a timely manner; therefore, frequent inspection is critical for early management, which stops problems from escalating.

Understand that one of the most crucial aspects of organic agriculture is record-keeping. It's critical to monitor your plants, their growth patterns, and any changes in soil composition or climate conditions.

This knowledge can help you make informed decisions about how to best care for your garden. Record-keeping can help discover patterns or problems early on, before they become too difficult to handle.

With these essentials in mind, you may start growing the organic garden of your dreams while simultaneously feeding your family nutritious vegetables.

Chapter 5
Growing A Naturally Healthy Organic Garden

You've attempted to eat more organic foods, both to limit the amount of chemicals you and your family consume and to help protect the environment.

However, as shown on your grocery receipt, organic foods can quickly become unreasonably expensive. Fortunately, organic gardening allows you to cultivate your own tasty, fresh produce while also having fun and learning!

Organic gardening eliminates the use of synthetic fertilizers and pesticides, but that does not mean your plants are left to fend for themselves.

There are numerous techniques available to help maintain plant health and avoid pest infestations. Begin on the right foot by ensuring that you have all of the necessary tools.

A quick recommendation for that beginner gardener

When first starting out, it is best to start small. Maybe your ultimate goal is to become completely self-sufficient. Perhaps you'd like to can and freeze vegetables so they can be stored for the entire winter.

While creating plans for the future is a terrific incentive, you should prioritize cultivating fresh food in your first garden so that you may eat it all summer.

Begin by learning the skills that you will need in the future. Growing a garden is a process; as the seasons change, you can experiment with new plants and approaches, expanding your knowledge as you physically grow your garden.

This year, focus on what you're learning, enjoy your time in the garden, keep track of the daily changes, and avoid placing too much pressure on yourself.

Selecting what to grow

According to Bioversity International's research, over 1,000 distinct types of vegetables have been planted around the world, yet less than 7% of these are grown on a consistent basis.

Due to the limited size of your garden bed, it's important to select appropriate plants.

There are a few options for reducing the list, but you will need to use common sense and make some difficult decisions. Take out a pencil and paper and begin listing items.

If you are a first-time gardener, choose simpler vegetable varieties that are suited to the growing circumstances in your area.

When should I start planting seeds?

Many plants, such as tomatoes, peppers, eggplants, and herbs, benefit from an early start to their growing season by being started indoors before moving them outside.

Generally, you should seed indoors six to eight weeks before your area's last frost date.

This gives your seedlings ample time to germinate, mature, and grow strong enough to be transplanted outside without being destroyed by extreme weather.

Remember that if you reside in a region with a longer growing season (such as California), you may not require as much advance time as someone in the Midwest or Northeast.

It also depends on the type of plant. Some seeds, such as pumpkins, germinate fast and do not require much of a head start, while others, such as celery, take 12 weeks or longer to germinate and must be started considerably earlier.

How to start seeds indoors

One of the most critical aspects of success when starting seeds indoors is selecting the appropriate container. While you may be tempted to use whatever container you have on hand, it is critical to utilize one built specifically for seed-starting.

These containers are often made of plastic or biodegradable materials, with drainage holes at the bottom. This is vital because drainage is essential for keeping your seedlings from becoming waterlogged, which can lead to disease and death.

This technique may vary slightly depending on the type of seed you are planting, so read any directions carefully and follow them exactly as written.

Most flower and vegetable seeds should be planted 1/4 inch deep, but some may demand a deeper planting depth. Once again, read the directions carefully! A decent general rule of thumb is to put seeds as deep as they are long.

Once planted, softly cover each seed with soil mix, but don't pack it down too firmly, as this can damage the fragile roots. As a bonus, identify each pot with a tag stating the type of seed within; this will save you time when transplanting!

Seedlings require warm temperatures, lots of light, and high humidity levels to thrive. If possible, use a heat mat to keep your seedlings warm and set them under grow lights for 14–16 hours per day.

You can also raise the humidity levels by placing a humidifier in the room or covering your seedlings with a clear plastic dome or bag. Simply remove the dome or bag periodically to allow your seedlings to breathe fresh air.

Once your seedlings have sprouted, it's critical to give them plenty of attention.

Water your seedlings near the base of the plant rather than from above. This can help prevent illnesses such as powdery mildew from spreading.

As the seedlings mature, you may need to trim them out (remove all except the strongest ones) and/or transplant them to larger containers. Most plants do this when they have two sets of true leaves.

How to plant seeds directly in your garden

Let's begin by prepping the soil where the seedlings will be planted. Dig a hole that is about twice as big and deep as the seedling's original pot, then add compost or fertilizer to give the plant a nutrient boost once transplanted outside.

Next, carefully remove each seedling from its pot and place it in the prepared hole, allowing plenty of space for the roots to expand.

Finally, fill in the area around the plant with dirt and properly water it to ensure a successful transition to its new environment!

Again, the size and type of seed you're planting will determine how deep you should plant it; smaller seeds should be placed shallower, while larger seeds should be planted deeper.

Most seed packets include information about planting depths, so read those directions carefully before planting!

Sow the larger seeds first, followed by the smaller ones, spacing them far enough apart to allow for growth when the sprouts appear.

Again, consult the seed packaging for specific instructions on how far apart your seeds should be spaced.

When you first start gardening, try to follow the guidelines on the seed packet as strictly as possible. As you gain more experience, you may want to try planting the seeds closer together.

In some circumstances, you may discover that this not only boosts plant yields but also reduces weed competition by leaving less open space between your cultivated plants for weeds to take hold.

However, do not do this until you are more seasoned and know exactly what to look for in terms of plant problem symptoms. It's also a good idea to wait until you have exceptionally fertile soil to ensure that your plants get everything they need.

It is also critical to ensure that all of the seeds are planted at the same depth; if some are placed too deep or too shallow, they may not germinate or survive once germinated.

Once all of the seeds have been planted, gently pat the soil surface with our hands and lightly water them with a watering can or hose attachment on a low-pressure setting (to avoid accidentally washing them away).

Do not overwater them, as this can cause rot and other problems in young plants.

When should you transplant the seeds you started inside?

If you live in a cold climate, wait until there is no danger of frost before planting your seedlings.

In most regions, this signifies late spring or early summer, typically two to three weeks following the last frost date.

If you live in a warm area, you may be able to begin transplanting as early as late in the winter or early in the spring.

Many gardeners make the mistake of transplanting their plants outside too quickly without giving them time to adjust to the new environment.

This is known as hardening off, and it is a critical stage that must not be overlooked if you want your plants to survive outside.

Hardening off is the process of gradually exposing your houseplants to the elements. The plant is gradually exposed to colder temperatures and brighter light until it can survive full sun and other outside situations.

The amount of time varies by plant species, but in general, plan on hardening off for about two weeks before planting in your garden or relocating indoors.

Hardening off allows plants to acclimate more slowly and safely to their new environment. It reduces the stress generated by abrupt temperature changes and intense sunlight, which can cause damage or even death in some plants.

It also allows immature seedlings to grow root systems that are strong enough to live outside with little care.

Without hardening off, plants may grow stunted or sickly due to a lack of nutrients or weak root systems that are unable to absorb water correctly.

As a general rule of thumb, start by exposing your plants to dappled sunlight outside for one hour every day, gradually increasing the amount of time spent outside over the course of two weeks until they can tolerate full sun exposure all day.

Check the soil moisture daily to ensure that the roots do not dry up too quickly in direct sunlight, especially on hot days when temperatures exceed 90 degrees Fahrenheit (32 degrees Celsius).

Misting with a spray bottle might help prevent drying up between watering sessions.

Keep an eye out for symptoms of stress, such as drooping leaves or discoloration, which may suggest that it's time to bring them back inside while they harden off for another day or two under milder circumstances.

Which vegetables on your list are suitable for the growing conditions you have?

Here are some things to consider:

1. How long—or short—is your growing season?
2. How much light does your garden receive on a daily basis?
3. The depth of your raised garden bed.
4. The size of your raised garden bed.

Which of these crops is easier to grow than the others?

Easiest to Grow	Medium	Hard
Beans (green, others)	Cantaloupe	Artichoke
Herbs (basil, hives, mint, oregano, and thyme)	Cucumbers	Broccoli
Kale	Peppers (hot or sweet)	Brussels sprouts
Leaf lettuce	Tomatoes	Cabbage
Onions, green		Carrots
Peas		Cauliflower
Potatoes		Celery
Radishes		Corn, sweet
Salad greens		Eggplant
Squash (especially yellow, zucchini)		Head lettuce
Swiss chard		Muskmelon
Turnips		Bulb onions
		Sweet potatoes
		Watermelon

Short-season vegetables are ideal for northern gardeners for succession planting.

Short-season vegetables (less than 120 days)

Beans, pole, snap (55 days to 70 days)	Beets (50 to 60 days)
Bok choy (30 to 60 days)	Broccoli (45 to 60 days)
Cabbage (100 days)	Carrots (60 to 80 days)
Cucumbers (50 days)	Eggplant (60 to 90 days)
Kale (55 days)	Lettuce, leaf (can be harvested when leaves are about 4 inches/10 centimeters in height)
Mustard, Mizuna, and Tatsoi (20 days)	Okra (50 days)
Green onions (40 to 50 days)	English peas (60 days)
Peppers (50 to 85 days)	New or fingerling potatoes (70 days)
Full-size potatoes (90 to 120 days)	Radishes (25 to 30 days)
Summer squash (40 to 60 days)	Cherry or grape tomatoes, small varieties (60 to 70 days)

Most vegetables demand full sunlight. Consider the following plants if your garden receives less sunlight than it should.

Vegetables for Light Shade
(these can also grow in the shade of taller plants).

Beans, pole, and fava	Beets
Broccoli	Brussels sprouts
Cabbage	Carrots
Cauliflower	Celery
Herbs (including borage, chervil, chives, cilantro, lemon balm, mints, oregano, parsley, perilla (or shiso), sorrel, tarragon, and thyme)	Kale
Leeks	Radishes
Rhubarb	Swiss chard
Turnips	

Raised Bed Depths

Less than 12 inches (30 cm) deep	12 to 18 inches (30 to 46 cm deep)	8 to 24 inches (46 to 61 cm) deep	24 to 36 inches (61 to 94 cm) deep
Chives	Previous plants and Arugula	Previous plants and beans dried, pole, and snap.	Previous plants and Artichokes
Lettuce	Bok Choy, Broccoli	Beets, Cantaloupe	Asparagus
Onions, green	Brussels sprouts	Carrots, Cucumber	Beans, lima
Radishes	Cabbage, Cauliflower	Eggplant, Kale	Okra, Parsnips
Salad greens	Celery, Corn	Peas, Peppers	Pumpkin, Rhubarb
Spinach	Endive, Garlic	Rutabagas	Squash, winter
	Kohlrabi	Spinach, summer	Sweet potatoes
	Onions, bulb	Sweet potatoes	Tomatoes
	Potatoes, Summer squash	Swiss chard	Watermelon

What is the maximum number of plants I can grow?

Consider the available area in your garden bed. Some plants, when fully grown, occupy a small space, but others are widespread and huge.

The size of the plants you choose will determine the kind and quantity of each plant you can grow.

When reading plant descriptions, seek out phrases like compact, bush, and dwarf, which indicate plants bred to leave a smaller imprint in the garden.

Depending on your preferences, you may choose to grow fewer and purchase larger vegetables rather than larger amounts of smaller varieties. The choice is yours.

Locate your plants

After you've selected your list of plants to grow, the next step is to decide which ones to purchase. As mentioned in earlier chapters, the majority of gardeners grow vegetables from seeds or bedding plants (sometimes called starts or transplants).

Seeds and bedding plants are commonly available online, in big-box stores, and in garden centers. Both have advantages and disadvantages, as well as reasons why one is preferable to the other.

Seeds

It's tremendously satisfying to harvest veggies from a plant you started from seed. If you open a seed catalog or visit one of the internet sites, you will note how many varieties are available for each vegetable.

For example, there are thousands of different tomato varieties. A large seed company may offer more than 50 kinds. In comparison, the garden center may only carry five or six distinct kinds of bedding plants.

Seeds can be grown in two ways: direct sowing and indoor beginning. Direct sowing is placing seeds in the garden in the exact location where they will grow during their life cycle.

It works better for plants with larger seeds and is appropriate for those with short growing seasons. Some plants may not thrive when their delicate roots are disturbed; they also do better when sown directly.

This approach can be problematic because it is highly dependent on the weather. If the weather is too cold or wet at the time of planting, the season may not be long enough for the plant to mature.

Seeds put directly in the garden are more susceptible to weed competition, as well as being eaten, washed, blown away, and dried out.

However, the seeds that survive these early shocks frequently grow into the toughest and most productive plants. Each variety of seed should be planted at the appropriate depth. They may not germinate if planted too deeply or not deep enough.

Large seeds typically have a depth that is three times their width. Smaller seeds typically only need to be pushed into the soil or lightly covered. To accommodate for losses, sow smaller seeds more thickly.

Once they germinate, you must thin them out by physically removing smaller or weaker seedlings to prevent crowding and competition.

Some other plants must be sown directly in the garden, but not from seeds.

Potatoes are grown from seed potatoes, which are tubers with developing roots. You can cut the potato into pieces, and as long as each piece has at least one eye through which a root grows, it will produce new potatoes. Allow potatoes with cut edges to dry for a few days before planting to avoid root rot.

Sweet potatoes are grown from slips (immature plants that sprout from a sweet potato), which you can purchase or grow yourself. Asparagus and rhubarb grow from bare root portions. Onions can be grown as seedlings, sets (small bulbs), or bedding plants.

Indoor seed starting is a preferable option for gardeners who have short growing seasons yet want to plant longer-season crops. It also works best for slow-growing plants and warm-season plants that do not grow in cool weather.

When starting seeds indoors, you have considerably more control over the growing circumstances, such as the start date, lighting, moisture, and temperature.

To decide the optimal time to start planting your seeds inside, refer to the final day of frost in your area as well as the days to maturity given on the seed packaging.

Plant your seeds four to eight weeks before the latest frost date. The idea is to get your plants between 3 and 6 inches (8 and 15 centimeters) tall during the appropriate outdoor planting period.

If you plant them too early and they don't get enough light, they can grow long and thin (or leggy). If you plant them too late, they may not be ready for planting in the garden at the appropriate time.

You should also allow about a week for it to harden off. Plants produced indoors are delicate because they have matured in regulated settings with little fluctuation.

As previously mentioned, hardening off is a procedure that prepares your plants for the harsher conditions of the garden, such as more light, fluctuating temperatures between day and night, and wind.

You begin the operation by placing your plants in a shady area away from the wind. Over the course of a week, progressively expose the plants to more direct sunlight and wind. By the end of the week, they should be strong enough to survive in the garden.

If you're simply planting a few seeds, a bright, sunny window sill with a southern exposure may have plenty of room and lighting.

For larger amounts of plants, more room and equipment will be required. Planting trays, pots, soilless seed-starting mixtures, extra lighting, bottom heating mats, fans, and hydrogen peroxide for disinfecting tools and workplaces are all common indoor seed-starting items.

Bedding plants

Bedding plants are similar to indoor seedlings, with the exception of the need for intermediaries. Wholesale transplant growers plant seeds in commercial operations and sell their plants to retail stores, who subsequently sell them to clients.

When they arrive in your local store, they are already several weeks old and ready to be planted in the garden as soon as the weather warms up. Purchasing bedding plants saves time, money, and hassle when compared to planting seeds.

When you bring your bedding plants home, you must harden them off, as mentioned above, unless the business where you got them has outside sales sections and the plants have already adapted to outdoor circumstances.

Once they have hardened off and the conditions are warm enough, you can remove them from their containers and plant them in the garden.

Direct seeding is ideal for arugula, beans, beets, carrots, corn, cucumbers, kale, kohlrabi, leaf lettuce, okra, onions, melons, parsnips, peas, radishes, rutabagas, spinach, summer squash (including zucchini), Swiss chard, and turnips.

Artichokes, basil, broccoli, Brussels sprouts, cabbage, cauliflower, celery, collards, eggplant, kale, kohlrabi, leeks, onions, peppers, scallions, tomatillos, and tomatoes are excellent choices for indoor seed starting or bedding plant purchases.

Seeds and bedding plants: A Comparison

When you plant seeds:

- You can buy seeds from organically grown plants.
- There is much more variety to choose from.
- It is more cost-effective; you get many more seeds for the same price as a bedding plant, but the initial setup for indoor seed starting can be costly.

- If seeds are sown directly, you won't have to worry about some plants suffering transplant shock and never recovering.

- You know exactly how each plant was cared for and what nutrients and chemicals were used as it grew.

- You don't have to worry about some plants, such as root erope, not developing properly after transplantation.

- Seeds make succession planting much easier. You do not have to go to the store to get more plants.

- There is no risk of introducing bugs into bedding plants.

- A suitable seed package requires less packaging than a plastic pot or cell tray.

- You have a sense of pride and personal satisfaction.

When you plant bedding plants:

- It is really convenient because much of the work has already been completed.

- They survived the vulnerable seeding stage.

- There is no need to purchase seed-starting supplies.

- Larger plants are less prone to pests and disease than tiny seedlings, but they are more susceptible to transplant shock.

- They may be overfertilized.

- Popular kinds may sell out rapidly, leaving you without the option you want.

ORGANIC GARDENING FOR BEGINNERS

- They are usually available for a limited time. They may not be available later in the season.

- They are not always well cared for later in the season. They may not be in optimal health.

- You can buy them at the time of planting.

- You can assess the health of the plant.

Reading a seed package

This may appear to be a simple task, but seed packets actually include a wealth of information for gardeners of all skill levels. Reading the fine print is very important in this scenario.

Each seed package should include all of the information you need to select and grow each plant. Unfortunately, there is no set structure; some vendors provide a lot of detail and great growing recommendations, while others don't.

At the very least, the package should contain:

- The plants are identified by both common and botanical names, as well as a variety or cultivar.

- The plant can be either annual, perennial, or biennial.

- Annuals' cold tolerance and perennials' hardiness zone.

- A physical description of the plant's growth habits and characteristics (vining, compactness, size, color, and so on).

- Sowing and growth conditions (light, moisture, planting time, days to maturity, days to germination, plant spacing, depth, pre-sowing, and sowing directions).

- Manufacture information (price, lot numbers, package size/quantity of seeds, day of manufacture).

Many packages include unique selling features, tips, and fascinating facts. A good image on the seed pack is beneficial, but it may be too expensive for small businesses.

New gardeners may be unfamiliar with some of the terms on seed packets. *Heirloom* seeds come from traditional plants that have been grown for generations or perhaps hundreds of years. All heritage plants are open-pollinated.

Plant breeders create *hybrid* seeds (or F1) in a controlled environment by cross-pollinating one variety with another to improve one or more plant features.

Hybrid plant seeds will not breed true; they will not resemble their hybrid parents and will instead revert to one of the "grandparent" plants. If you want to save and grow seeds from your own plants for future gardens, don't buy hybrid seeds.

Open-pollinated seeds (OP) come from plants that are naturally pollinated by bees, butterflies, and the wind. You can collect seeds from these plants; they will have the same features as the parent plant and will reproduce properly.

The round green and white USDA Organic label verifies that the seeds were grown with "natural substances and physical, mechanical, or biologically based farming methods" (McEvoy, 2017). This does not imply that no pesticides are used in their production; rather, organic insecticides are employed.

Genetically modified (GMO) seeds have been extensively covered in the media. They are quite contentious, yet they are only employed in the commercial agriculture business. GMO seeds are not available for home garden use.

A friendly reminder for beginning gardeners

When starting a garden for the first time, there is a lot to learn, and it takes longer than you expect. Your aim is to succeed in growing a naturally healthy organic garden, and all of your decisions should be geared toward guaranteeing your success—as much as that is possible.

Using bedding plants in your garden is a great way to get gardening experience without having to invest time or money in seed-growing.

But in late winter, I strongly advise you to start and grow one vegetable from seed right in the garden or in a sunny window. It's a fulfilling and reaffirming experience to grow something from seeds, especially if you have children.

Sunflowers, radishes, nasturtiums, and beans all grow easily and germinate quickly. Fostering a child's interest in gardening is a great way to spend quality time together, and it's never too early.

Honestly, it doesn't really matter how long you have been gardening; whether you are planning your 40th or first garden, the new season serves as a reminder to start again and learn from all of your past mistakes.

Chapter 6
Making Use of Natural Resources

Natural resources include water, earth, wind, and sun. With a little preparation and understanding, you can make the most of these resources for your garden.

In order to lessen waste, promote the growth of our garden, and benefit the environment, we can capture and store their energy.

We'll discuss how to employ the sun, wind, and water collecting in this chapter.

Collecting of rainwater

Collecting rainwater is one of the most effective and simple things you can do to improve your garden. Rainwater harvesting or catchment refers to the collection and storage of rainwater from a structure's runs.

A gray water collection system, which includes pumps, tanks, and filters, can be as simple as a barrel placed beneath your gutter drain spout or as complicated as an extensive system.

Water is in constant motion across the world. It is constantly changing forms in a process termed the hydrologic cycle. Precipitate, gather, evaporate, and condense multiple times.

In more technical words, the "collect" stage is the process by which surface runoff from rain enters ponds, rivers, and seas.

Many people have the misperception that there is not enough water in their location. However, it is more of a collection shortage. The idea is to capture the water as it goes through its cycle.

Several rainwater collection systems have been widely successful around the world, including imprinting, trincheras, gabions, and the Vallerani system.

However, attempting to condense them into a single chapter may cause us mental anguish. So, for the time being, let's keep things simple.

Rain barrels provide a natural solution

Rainwater is an ideal natural resource to capture. It's completely free! It's also full of minerals and nutrients that your plants will appreciate. And collecting it benefits the ecosystem by reducing pollution in rivers, lakes, and streams.

For example: A 1,000-square-foot roof may capture 20,000 gallons of water per year. So, how do we capture all of this free water? It's a simple rain barrel that's ideal for a beginner gardener.

As mentioned before, rain barrels collect rainwater that falls from the roof and store it for later use. They can be installed with faucets, allowing you to use the water as needed.

A rain barrel can be purchased online, at a local home and garden store, or through the local municipality. Alternatively, you can make your own. You will just need a few basic things from a home improvement store or garden center.

Online classifieds such as Craigslist frequently list 55-gallon barrels for sale. You could also use an old wooden wine barrel or a huge plastic trash can with a lid.

And if you just want to get started and test anything, place a 5-gallon bucket where most of the rain falls from your roof during the next storm. As the clouds clear, you'll get 5 gallons of rain that you wouldn't have otherwise.

Your rain barrel should be put at the base of an existing downspout on your house, garage, barn, or other outbuilding. The location should be flat, and the barrel should be raised a few feet off the ground to make it easier to pour water.

You'll probably need to alter your downspout so that water flows into the rain barrel's entrance. You should have a drainage pipe installed to divert overflow. This could be located in your garden or in another rain barrel.

Make sure your rain barrel has a screen over the intake to keep debris and mosquitoes out. Rain barrels require little maintenance once installed. Use the water as needed to empty the barrel in time for the next rainstorm.

Inspect your rain barrels on a monthly basis to maintain their security.

To avoid freezing, many barrels must be drained and stored upside down throughout the winter months.

Build a swale to slow, spread, sink, and store water

What is the use of a swale? Swales are among the most often used stormwater strategies.

For many years, they have been utilized to transport runoff from rural roadways and residential streets.

Today, swales not only transport stormwater but also aid in treating runoff and minimizing contaminants.

That being said, swales are one of the best ways to "catch and store" this strong rain energy directly in the soil.

You can accomplish this by utilizing the way water flows across your property and deliberately redirecting it where you want it to go.

Not only does this ease drainage and erosion issues, but it also feeds and rehydrates the soil. Unless your property has been carefully landscaped, rainwater will pool wherever nature (and gravity) directs it.

Entire books might be written about strategic rainwater redirection. We mentioned a few water systems above, but here are some more, for all you researchers:

Storm runoff can be managed using a variety of methods, including French drains, infiltration basins, sunken garden beds, keylines, and waffle beds.

Swales and berms are perhaps the most common approach you'll hear about. These terms are likely to be used as frequently as "natives" and "perennials" in everyday conversations.

These earthworks techniques have numerous advantages: they handle erosion and drainage problems, catch and store energy to feed the soil, hydrate the land, create edges and microclimates, and are excellent locations to grow things.

Because there is so much to say about earthworks, I will only cover the fundamentals here.

As previously stated, a swale is a broad, shallow canal at the base of a slope used to direct and store runoff. In layman's terms, a ditch.

If you reside in an area without sidewalks, you may notice swales along the sides of the street.

Swales are commonly vegetated, which means that plants grow in them.

Water rushes down the slope and accumulates in the swale. This gives water to the plants growing in the swale, the slope leading down to it, the berm on the opposite side, and the area beyond the berm.

A berm is a small artificial mound or bank constructed from soil.

Swales are ideal for planting water-loving plants, brushes, fruit, and nut trees, as well as a variety of perennials and herbs. The berm on the other side produces a great no-till bed.

Optimizing plant choices for different areas on a swale and berm system requires some thought, depending on your environment.

Learn how to use swales and direct flow to get the most out of your water

So, how can you build a swale to direct the flow of rainfall in your garden? It only takes some thoughtful digging. There are a few factors to keep in mind when constructing a swale.

First and foremost, swales and berms are intended to do more than just reroute water around your property. They may assist you in changing your water flow from erosive to non-damaging, strategic, and mild.

Swales and berms are both planting systems. They are intended to catch and hold water in appropriate locations so that it can slowly sink into the soil and nourish it as well as neighboring plants. It's like a slow-release water pill for your garden.

On a side note, the amount of organic matter in your property's soil has a significant impact on its water retention capacity. The more organic matter you incorporate into the soil, the more water it will retain.

Swales do not solve all drainage concerns. You will need to carefully watch how water flows on your property and plan where you want to install swales and berms. Water gathered in a swale soaks into the region below the berm and drains downhill.

The subterranean well you're building is known as the water plume. Every year, this plume grows. It permeates a larger region beneath the surface, replenishing underground aquifers and plants further away from the swale.

When digging a swale, there are a few factors to consider. The trench should be level throughout its length so that water does not pool in any one area.

Also, with this subsurface plume in mind, you can understand why a swale at the bottom of your slope wouldn't do much to hydrate your yard (though it would assist with drainage concerns).

For this reason, digging a swale at a high point while keeping it low enough to catch runoff is ideal. Basically, it is uphill from the garden. In fact, on bigger properties, numerous swales are constructed, with gardens and guilds in between.

Considerations for swale safety

When building a swale, there is a chance that the slope will be extremely steep, and because we are working with dirt, most of us are aware that water may be a very powerful and destructive force.

Swales and berms are not suggested for slopes greater than 15 degrees (about 1:3.75). Landslides can occur on steeper slopes. Swales should have a grade of 3 to 15 degrees.

There are a few more key structural notes. Swales should be at least 10 feet away from buildings, and water should constantly flow away from them.

Also, the top 8 inches of soil in the swale should be well-drained. Water should not remain in the swale for longer than a few days.

Finally, you'll want some overflow passages in case it rains heavily. At the swale's ends, simply cut through the berms about 3/4 of the way up to direct the water to another location. This might potentially be the next swale down the slope.

Building the berms

What do we do with all of the soil we dug out when making our swales?

The best thing you can do is utilize the soil to form a berm on the other side of the swale. Simply mound up the soil on the downhill side of the swale over its whole length.

I certainly recommend looking out how-tos to obtain some ideas for estimating dimensions and devising designs that are perfect for your specific situation.

Swales are typically 18 inches to 2 feet wide, 6 inches to 1.5 feet deep, and as long as they can be dug. However, swales differ in each space.

Planting on berms and swales

It's a good idea to plant on the berm as soon as the swale is finished, especially with ground cover (legumes, for example) on top.

This would reduce erosion and help keep soil in place. It would also start amending the soil in preparation for the other plants you plan to grow on the berm.

What you plant depends on your climate. Those from drier areas may grow extensively in the swale itself to maximize the use of the pooled water.

Those from wetter areas may prefer water-loving plants in the swale and use different parts of the swale and berm hillsides for different purposes.

This method is commonly employed for long-term perennials, which are planted in guilds on the berm to maximize the use of the water plume.

When planted on or directly below the swale, more firmly rooted perennials, such as nut trees, help to keep the system in place. Smaller plants and trees are ideal for the sides of the berm.

Other perennials and herbs are grown uphill from the swale. Annual gardens are frequently positioned downhill from the perennial guilds, beyond the berm.

Making use of the water plume as it expands. When you examine the variety of microclimates formed by this system, you have a lot of options.

Some will utilize this technique as the foundation for their food forest, filling in all of the layers in various locations: uphill from the swale, inside the swale, on top of the berm, on the sides, downhill, and so on. This is stacking at its finest.

Building a hügel mound

What precisely is a hügel mound? A hügel mound is literally translated as "hill culture" and is derived from the German word 'hügelkultur'. Sepp Holzer pioneered the technique, which entails creating a raised bed filled with rotten wood and other waste items to create an extremely productive soil.

However, before you begin developing a hügel, you should analyze its advantages and disadvantages before combining functions.

Huguls are commonly used for annuals and short-term perennials because they are meant to decompose and collapse on themselves over time. A swale is designed to be a more permanent mound for a longer-term perennial system.

It's not impossible to install a swale in front of a massive mound, but the key here is to conduct research and plan beforehand. Otherwise, you may run into problems later on.

If you used hugelkultur with larger logs and followed a deeply dug swale on a very steep slope, you could end up with a log slide after heavy rain.

So, when working with swales, get to know your surroundings, do some digging (figuratively rather than practically), and ask questions. If you want to understand more about Hugel's, do a simple Google search for "Hugelkultur swales.".

When to use swales

Depending on your specific geography, climate, or other unique characteristics, they may not be the best example. If your grade is steeper, you may want to consider terracing or another approach.

Also, if your land is already quite moist, you may not require swales, which are designed to replenish groundwater and hydrate the soil.

What you may do is utilize a different type of swale—a diversion ditch—that is inclined rather than flat across the length and is intended to redirect water to another location, such as a pond or rain garden.

Hopefully, this information will help you understand how and when to utilize this tool. As you explore how to harness the rain on your land, there is another strategic consideration:

Observe your surroundings and plant strategically

Rainwater can be used to your advantage by carefully studying your surroundings and strategically planting. Some plants enjoy having damp feet. This means that their root systems can tolerate constantly wet circumstances.

Plant thirsty plants in areas where rainwater is abundant or flows more freely, such as near the foot of a hill or a low point on your property. These plates will collect moisture and keep it from running off into other regions.

Many plant species prefer damp soil. Wetland flora include chokeberry, pussywillow, marsh marigold, Joe Pye weed, hibiscus, cardinal flower, and giant elephant ears.

If you have a dry location in your yard, plant drought-tolerant plants. Swamp milkweed, butterfly weed, goldenrod, Indian tobacco, trumpet honeysuckle, and a few native trees are other examples.

The remaining elements of your space

While water and earth are garden heroes, there are two additional elements that are quite beneficial: wind and sunlight. These natural resources are at work in your garden every day, and utilizing their potential is simply a matter of careful planning.

Harnessing the wind

The wind is an excellent resource for pollination, distributing seeds and pollen that might otherwise remain close to the parent plant. It provides the resistance that immature plants require to form strong stems.

Positioning your garden beds in areas with good air circulation also helps to avoid disease. Some even build wind turbines (of various sizes and complexity levels) to transform the air into electricity.

However, excessive wind might have a negative impact on the plants. Strong gusts can harm foliage, ruin blooms, displace unripe fruit, and reduce cold and moisture levels.

If you are working in a windy area, building a windbreak can help safeguard your plants.

A windbreak is a construction that prevents wind from entering a certain location. It can be natural or man-made. Manmade windbreaks can take the form of fences or building walls.

If you have a little more room, natural windbreaks such as hedges, bushes, and trees are a great way to add green beauty to your landscape. Native hedge plants, in particular, encourage wildlife and defend your yard.

Alternatively, you can combine the two by creating a structure that plants can climb.

Create a wall with reinforced mesh, lattice, or bamboo canes. Then, plant vining plants such as ivy, honeysuckle, or Virginia creeper and let them cover the structure.

Aside from appearing stunning, this offers a semi-permeable windbreak that is more effective than a full wall.

And in an urban area, this green wall serves as excellent privacy screening from nosy neighbors.

You can also apply this method on a balcony or patio; simply plant your vines in pots.

Soak up the sun

Solar power is an environmentally beneficial and efficient way to power your home.

There are incredible ways to harness the sun's continual power, ranging from passive solar to active systems.

On a smaller scale, solar-powered outdoor lights and pumps for water features are viable options.

However, until you receive that government grant for roof-mounted solar panels, you may benefit from the sun in your organic garden by watching how it moves across your property.

Which areas received the highest and least quantity of sunlight? How many hours of sunlight will your garden get?

If you haven't before, apply this knowledge to each plant in your intended plan.

If you're not sure how much sunlight a plant needs on a daily basis, check the back of the seed packet or the ID tag on a store-bought seedling.

When planning your plot, consider the maturity height of your plants, especially if you are companion planting.

Always place tall plants on the north side of the garden and shorter plants on the south side.

This allows them all to absorb enough light when the sun moves across the sky.

Conclusion: With the force of the elements behind you, you're soaking up the sun, controlling the wind, sculpting the earth, and harvesting the rain.

There is absolutely nothing that may prevent you from creating the organic garden of your dreams!

Chapter 7
Composting and Recycling Used Trash

Whether it's learning how to upcycle old rubbish, compost kitchen waste, or find the hidden power of weeds, as a beginner gardener, you must understand how to transform "trash" into beautiful treasure.

As a new gardener, you never want a resource to leave your property without being used effectively.

Examine your surroundings. Nature has so much to offer: the leaves fall, decay, and fertilize the soil.

Forest soil is rich, and compost is the best and most natural approach to providing nutrients to your crop.

The Alchemy of composting: A guide to reducing waste

Composting is the process of converting organic waste into plant food. Anything that was once alive naturally decays through decomposition. Beneficial bacteria, fungus, worms, and other microscopic animals aid in this breakdown.

When the composting process is complete, we refer to the product as finished, mature, or stable compost. This indicates it is ready for use in your garden.

As organic matter degrades into compost, it activates the three major macronutrients, NPK (Nitrogen N, Phosphorus P, and Potassium K), which are required for plant growth.

It stores these nutrients (and others) and delivers them consistently to the plant's root system. It improves soil quality and fertility. It improves water retention. It makes the Earth happy.

So, can plants grow in straight compost? Not really.

Although compost provides all of the nutrients that plants require, it lacks the soil structure that allows it to retain water and maintain stability. Some low-spreading, acid-loving plants, such as squash, can grow in compost alone.

However, most plants prefer a balanced combination. Compost should be added as a topdressing layer in garden beds, about 1-3 inches deep. Alternatively, you can mix it into the soil at a rate of 10%–25%.

What can and cannot be composted?

Almost any organic (alive) matter can be composted. This includes cooking waste and yard debris.

However, some items can cause problems if discarded in the compost heap. E. coli, salmonella, and listeria bacteria can contaminate waste like meat and dog excrement (as well as dung from other carnivores).

This, in turn, may infect the entire batch of compost. It increases the chance of transferring bacteria to your plants. These materials can also attract rats and give your compost an unpleasant odor.

However, these items can be composted separately in a pile designated specifically for landscaping. It's an excellent way to dispose of all that dog excrement. Just don't put it on anything you plan to eat.

A list of dos and don'ts for composting

Here are a few lists of products to compost, divided into green materials (nitrogen-rich) and brown materials (carbon-rich). Then, develop a more detailed inventory of the products you do not compost.

Finally, there are some notes on certain products with special considerations.

Do compost

Green (nitrogen-rich)

Alfalfa, algae, clover, coffee grounds, food scraps (vegetables, etc.), feathers, fresh plant cuttings and flowers, grains, grass clippings, hair and fur, hedge clippings, jams, jellies, preserves, manure (herbivores only; see below), nail clippings, old spices, seaweed, lakeweed, kelp, soybean meal, sprouts, stale bread, tea leaves, tofu, water from a freshwater aquarium, wine, beer, and spirits.

Browns (carbon-rich)

Ashes (wood), bark, bedding from herbivore pins (rabbits, chickens, etc .), burlap, cardboard, coffee filters, and tea bags (only natural materials), corks, cotton and wool fabrics like towels, sheets, and clothes (100% natural fibers), dead dried plants and grass, dead leaves, egg cartons (biodegradable), lint and dust, loofahs (natural), paper material (see note below), nut shells, parchment paper, pasta and rice (not if cooked with oil or meat), pencil shavings, pine needles.

Middle ground in composting

Some items are nitrogen-rich when fresh but become carbon-rich when dried. Sometimes they fall somewhere in the middle.

Corn cobs and stalks, eggshells, fruit debris, ruined hay, a large amount of garden waste, and plant and weed cuttings. These are wonderful examples of products that fall somewhere between being composted and not.

Do NOT Compost

In general, you should avoid adding the following materials to your compost:.

Coal ash, charcoal, bioplastics, black walnut products, bones, cellophane, chemically treated wood, sawdust, charcoal, cigarettes, coated cardboard and glossy paper (see note below on paper), dairy products, diapers (see not below), diseased or contaminated plants (see below), excrement from carnivores or humans, foil, glass, grasses with roots that spread under the soil, produce labels, leather goods, meat, seafood products, metal, Netting from fruit, oils and grease (see below), plastic, styrofoam, synthetic fabrics, synthetic soaps, wax paper, and weeds that have gone to seed (see weed note below).

Special considerations:

Bread

Some argue that baked products attract pests. However, if it is edible, it can be composted. It is ideal to use stale bread that has been torn into smaller pieces, thrown into the center of the mound, and covered.

Citrus peels, onions, and garlic

Many people will advise you not to include too many of these ingredients in your compost. Yes, they are acidic and, in theory, can increase the acidity of your compost.

However, unless you own a lemon farm, you're probably fine. Composting Magazine (2023a). However, when it comes to vermicomposting (with worms), you may want to limit them (see below).

Oils

Again, oils are frequently on the naughty list for composting because they can make your pile smell bad and attract bugs. Of course, an unavoidable, minor amount (such as residual grease on a pizza box) isn't too bad.

Furthermore, some studies suggest that cooking oils may benefit the composting process (Composting Magazine 2023b). Try hot composting, dumping it in the center, and covering it up.

Paper

Paper is ideal for the compost pile. Worms enjoy it, too. In general, avoid glossy, waxy, or coated paper, as well as magazines.

Manure

The usual rule of thumb is to exclusively use herbivore excrement. In general, you should avoid using feces from predatory animals, pets (dogs, cats), and humans.

However, if you wish to compost any of them, it will require a little research and is generally best done in a separate bin.

While we're on the topic:

Diapers, sanitary products, toilet paper, etc

Compostable diapers, feminine hygiene products, and other options are available for individuals who are interested. Again, do your research. FYI: Wet diapers are easier to compost than #2 diapers, for the obvious reasons stated above.

Weeds and plant matter

Weeds can be composted, but there are a few methods to make the most of their utilization. Most infections can be removed using hot composting methods.

If you are willing to accept the risk, employ an "experimental" pile (see below). It's preferable to avoid chemically contaminated plants, though.

Vermicomposting and worm food

You can generally follow all of the guidelines above, with a few changes:

Avoid onions, garlic, citrus, peppers, animal products, carnivore and "hot" manure, spices, and fried, salty, or oily foods.

Limit bread and grains, and use coffee grounds sparingly. Allow grass clippings to dry slightly before putting them in hot and fresh water (they can heat up quickly), and keep eggshells dry and crushed.

As previously stated, worms enjoy paper, but not glossy or coated paper. Just a few tips.

A small deviation from the rules

Animals in the wild eventually perish and decompose; this is a natural process. That being said, here are some more composting recommendations.

If you wish to use the dairy, meat, cooking oil, and dog feces, create a separate compost pile for non-edible plants (such as landscaping).

Put all of your "experimental" materials in this pile. It is better to construct a heated compost pile to kill disease and weed spores.

To keep pests away, bury experimental materials (meat, dairy, oils, etc.) under standard materials (leaves, sawdust).

Still, certain materials do not degrade (such as plastic) or should be handled in a commercial composting facility (such as polluted plants), but most "natural" items can be composted.

In general, whether anything is edible or decomposes, it will most likely compost over time.

Composting ratios

At the end of the day, you're probably fine with simply estimating your "greens and browns" balance, checking in on the pile periodically, and adjusting as needed.

The charts below can help you understand how to balance your compost.

Some greens contain more nitrogen than others. Some browns contain more carbon than others. With that in mind, greens and browns have been divided into three simple categories, each with a "score.".

The goal is simple: keep the score even.

Food scraps, for example, are a "low" nitrogen green with a score of -1. Sawdust is a high-carbon brown with a +3. That implies one handful of sawdust may equal three handfuls of food scraps.

Alternatively, if you add two handfuls of food scraps, balance them with one handful of shredded paper. You can also exchange 1 handful of leaves for 1 handful of kitchen waste.

Keep in mind that this will not be exact, but it may help you obtain a general idea of things.

GREEN MATERIALS

C:N NITROGEN BALANCE	COMPOSTING INGREDIENTS
-1 ...... LOW (> 20:1)	FOOD SCRAPS, COFFEE GROUNDS, TEA LEAVES, MANY PLANT CUTTINGS.
-2 ...... MED (12:1 - 20:1)	GRASS CLIPPINGS, LEGUMES, LEAFY GREEN VEGETABLES, SEAWEED.
-3 ...... HIGH (5:1 - 12:1)	HAIR, FUR, SOYBEAN MEAL, MANY FRESH MANURES.

BROWN MATERIALS

C:N CARBON BALANCE	COMPOSTING INGREDIENTS
+1 ..... LOW (< 60:1)	DRIED LEAVES, NUT SHELLS, CORN COBS, WOOD ASH
+2 ..... MED (75:1 - 200:1)	STRAW, CORN STALKS, PINE NEEDLES, SHREDDED PAPER
+3 ..... HIGH (300:1 +)	SAWDUST, WOOD CHIPS, SHREDDED CARDBOARD

Chapter 8

The Organic Solution to Weed and Pest Control

I know most people despise weeding; call me odd, but I find it somewhat therapeutic. So when I see a weed in my garden, I pull it right away. Pulling the occasional weed from the garden is simple; waiting until the area is covered in weeds is discouraging.

Did you realize that weeds as a concept did not exist until the 1950s? When synthetic herbicides were invented and introduced, plants that were previously considered weeds became the enemy. It appears that the development of a weed-eliminating product exacerbated the problem (Timmons, 1970).

What exactly is a weed?

Ralph Waldo Emerson, a 19th-century American philosopher and writer, may have argued that "a weed is but a plant whose virtues remain undiscovered" (Ralph Waldo Emerson, 1878), yet most gardeners agree that weeds are not welcome in their gardens, undiscovered virtues or not.

So, what is it about these plants that makes them so hated?

A weed is any plant that grows in an area where it was not intentionally planted and is unwanted. Most weeds have several traits.

- Weeds produce tremendous amounts of seed.
- The seeds are frequently quite tiny.
- Weed seed germinates quickly.
- There is a high viability percentage (the majority of seeds generated germinate and thrive).
- Seeds can remain viable even after lying dormant for extended periods of time.
- Seeds frequently have physical characteristics that help them spread widely (burrs, fluff).

Green foxtail is an annual grass that can be extremely harmful to cats and dogs.

When the seed head matures, individual seeds develop sharp barbs that stick to pets as they pass by. The barbs can become lodged in the pet's paws, ears, nose, throat, and genitalia.

Foxtail barbs (or awns) can centralize and migrate throughout the animal's body, and they have been discovered during necropsy in a variety of internal organs, including the lungs and brain.

A single foxtail plant can generate up to 500 seeds per head, and each plant may have ten heads (Gervase, 2018).

Chickweed is another weed that produces an abundance of seeds. A single chickweed plant can generate 10,000 to 20,000 seeds every season (Gervase, 2018).

How much do weeds really grow?

Weeds may endure a wide range of soil types (nutrient-deficient, acidic, alkaline, sandy, and clay) and environmental conditions.

Some weeds have evolved protective characteristics (thorns, hairy leaves, and stems; toxicity; noxious sap) to keep them from being devoured.

Some weeds are allelopathic, meaning they produce compounds that kill or impede competing plants. Under ideal conditions, some weeds can grow 1 to 2 inches (2.5 to 5 centimeters) overnight after germination. Most vegetable seedlings cannot grow at this rate.

Weed seedlings suck a considerable amount of nutrients from the soil as they grow quickly, leaving little for the young crop.

As it grows, the weed protects the vegetable from sunlight. Without sunlight, photosynthesis cannot occur, and seedlings will not have enough energy to grow.

Kudzu, an invasive vining perennial weed, was introduced to the United States at the Philadelphia Centennial Fair in 1876. I was touted as a decorative plant, livestock feeding, and erosion-controlling cover crop.

During the 1930s and 1940s, the US government delivered 85 million seedlings and paid farmers to plant the vine. Kudzu has now spread throughout the southeastern United States and is classified as a noxious weed in some states.

Kudzu can grow up to 60 feet (18 meters) per season (Southern Living, 2018).

Weeds have large root systems

Weeds have two main types of root systems. Some push their roots deep into the soil, creating a taproot that is nearly impossible to pull out without breaking.

Other weeds spread their roots laterally. When parts break off, new plants might grow from the fractured root remnants.

Bindweed is a perennial vine with roots that can stretch up to 14 feet (4 meters) underground. Bindweed roots can develop for 50 years without apparent foliage before sprouting above the ground (Gervase, 2018).

The distinction among introduced, invasive, and noxious

Weeds can be classified into several groups based on their environmental impact. An imported species is one that has entered the country, either unintentionally or intentionally. After being introduced, it has the potential to become either invasive or beneficial.

An invasive species, which includes not only plants but also animals, birds, fungi, and bacteria, is one that is not native to the ecosystem and has the potential to harm the environment, the economy, or human health. Invasive species compete with and eliminate native species (National Conservation Service, n.d.).

A noxious species may be invasive, non-invasive, introduced or native. The distinction involved an impact that could endanger the environment, human health, agriculture, natural resources, navigation, or recreation (National Resources Conservation Service, n.d.).

Weed-like plants

Although they are not typically considered weeds, some plants behave aggressively in a garden and can successfully act like weeds given the correct growing conditions.

Some of these plants spread by their roots, while others spread through seeds or both. If these plants are hybrids, the plants that produce seeds will not have the same qualities as the parent plants, which may be undesirable.

Always grow mint family plants (including peppermint and spearmint) in pots so that their roots do not spread. Other spreaders include catnip, bee balm, lemon balm, thyme, dill, calendula, chamomile, chives, parsley, and oregano.

Do you know how to identify a plant in the mint family? Feel the stem; if it is square in shape, it is a mint.

Weed removal

If you are constructing a new raised bed garden and the area where you want to place it is already occupied by weeds and grass, you may want to remove them to prevent them from entering your garden.

It may be tempting to go to the big box store and buy a container of pesticide, but the World Health Organization has designated glyphosate and polyethoxylated tallow amine as probable human carcinogens (Van Bruggen et al., 2018).

Glyphosate herbicides operate systemically rather than topically. When sprayed on the plant, it absorbs and spreads to the leaves, stems, and roots.

Studies have demonstrated that glyphosate herbicides, such as Roundup, are particularly harmful to bees.

After you've prepared your garden bed and sown your seeds, regular maintenance is required to keep your garden on track to produce the healthy harvests you've been hoping for. General maintenance guidelines are mentioned throughout this book.

However, you will most likely find it beneficial to have access to these in a single chapter that can be used as a reference for understanding how to maintain your garden and the tools used to work in it.

The poisonous compounds hinder the bees' ability to locate nectar and pollen and return to their colonies (Balbuena et al., 2015).

The techniques listed below are effective, sustainable, and safe.

Solarization

Solarization employs the sun's heat to eliminate weeds, pests, and soil-borne diseases.

To solarize your garden:

1. Begin by cutting the weeds and grass as short as possible.

2. Water the area thoroughly.

3. Spread clear plastic over the soil's surface, secure it with bricks or landscape staples, or bury the edges.

4. Make a tight seal around the edges of the plastic.

Solarization works best in areas that receive 6 to 8 hours of direct sunlight every day. The tarp should be left in place for 2 to 6 weeks, depending on the temperature.

You can also employ solarization to kill weed seeds before planting in an existing raised bed; this is especially successful when the raised bed frame is filled with new soil. The plastic can be stapled straight onto the frame.

Cardboard Sheet Mulching

Cardboard sheet mulching is a simple, inexpensive, and effective way to remove weeds before establishing a raised bed garden.

As with solarization, keep weeds and grass as short as possible. If the ground is hard, saturate it completely.

If you're using cardboard boxes, remove any tape and glossy labels first, then cut along the box's seam to open it up. Place the cardboard over the garden bed, overlapping the sheets generously.

At least 6 to 8 inches (15 to 22 cm). Once the entire garden has been covered in cardboard, water it thoroughly. Use pegs and bricks to anchor the cardboard to the ground. The raised bed frame can be positioned on top of the cardboard.

Place a layer of weed chips over the cardboard in the frame, then add your soil, and it's ready to plant. This method can also be used to create a weed barrier under mulch or gravel pathways going to and around the bed.

As the cardboard decomposes, it promotes good soil and attracts earthworms, who appear to have a special fondness for cardboard.

Weed prevention

Weeds are best controlled by preventing them from growing in the first place.

Mulching

Covering exposed soil with heavy layers of mulch prevents weeds from sprouting and developing.

Remove flowers

Each flower that blooms can produce hundreds or thousands of weed seeds. By removing the flowers before they mature, none of the seeds will germinate. Please throw seed heads in the garbage rather than in your composter.

Composters must reach 145 degrees Fahrenheit (63 degrees Celsius) for 30 days to effectively destroy seeds.

Unless you routinely monitor the temperature in your composting bin, it is difficult to confirm that the desired temperatures have been reached and that the seeds are no longer viable for growth. (Weed Science Society of America, 2009).

No tilling or limited tilling

Because weed seeds can remain latent in the soil for long periods of time, using a no-till or limited-tilling technique limits the number of times seeds are exposed to germination-friendly circumstances.

Tight spacing

When you start planting your garden, pay attention to the spacing recommendations on the seed packages or bedding plant labels to determine how much area the mature plant requires.

Use these measures to arrange your plants so that the entire garden is covered with green. Weed seeds germinate less readily when the soil is less exposed.

Infill planting

Infill planting is a good weed reduction approach. Look for random, vacant spots in your garden where you can put another veggie or a companion plant to help repel pests.

Careful fertilization and irrigation

When watering or applying compost or fertilizer, make sure to target the plants you want to grow rather than those you don't. Targeted treatments save money, supplies, labor, and time spent on weeding.

Imported weeds

Every time you buy soil, compost, or bedding plants, there's a chance you'll also get a few weeds. If there are visible weeds in a potted vegetable, eliminate them before transplanting it to your garden.

For the first few weeks, keep an eye out for the appearance of weed seedlings in the soil and remove them as soon as possible.

Weed control methods: Chemical herbicide alternatives

Hand-pulling

Hand-pulling weeds is one of the simplest techniques to control weeds, and it works best when the soil is moist and the weed is still juvenile. Hold the stem near the weed's base and carefully pull it from the soil.

The goal is to remove the entire plant, including the roots, but many weeds break off before the roots are freed. It will grow back, but each time you pull it, you reduce photosynthesis and the weed's capacity to generate energy for growth.

If you don't let the stems and leaves develop, the weed will finally die.

Boiling water

Boiling water can be helpful in killing weeds, especially those that grow between pavement cracks or brick pavers.

It will only kill the foliage above ground; a single application will not kill the root and must be repeated.

Take extra precautions when transporting a kettle to avoid spraying it on yourself or plants that you want to protect.

Vinegar/salt solution

- 1 gallon (3.79 liters) vinegar
- 8 ounces (227 grams) salt
- 0.5-ounce (15-milliliter) dish soap

Combine all of the ingredients in a big container or bucket and mix thoroughly. Use a funnel to transfer the solution to a spray bottle. Saturate the weeds with the solution. Any plant sprayed with this solution will be affected.

Vinegar's active component is acetic acid. It absorbs all of the moisture from the plant's leaves, drying them out.

The salt in the combination enhances the drying effect. The dish soap functions as a wetting agent, allowing the vinegar and salt to remain on the leaf for longer and soak more thoroughly.

Vinegar can be purchased with varying levels of acetic acid, up to 20%, which is more harmful to the plant. If you use higher doses, you must take extra measures when handling them.

Wear goggles and gloves, and avoid inhaling the fumes when mixing and applying.

Alcohol-based solution

- 2-ounces (59 milliliters) of rubbing alcohol or inexpensive vodka
- 16 ounces (473 milliliters) water
- 3-4 drops of dish soap

Mix the contents in a spray bottle and apply to the weeds. The alcohol solution, like the vinegar-salt solution, dries out the plant tissues.

Baking soda solution

- 12 ounces (340 grams) baking soda
- 1 ounce (30 mL) of vinegar
- 1-gallon (3.79 liters) of water
- 3-4 drops of dish soap

Combine these materials in a container or bucket. Use a funnel to transfer the solution to a spray bottle. Saturate any plants you want to get rid of.

Lemon juice and vinegar

- 8 ounces (250 milliliters) of lemon juice
- 8 ounces (250 milliliters) of vinegar
- 3-4 drops of dish soap

Combine the ingredients in a spray bottle. Spray the solution on the weeds. Lemon juice includes citric acid, which functions by burning plant leaves. These methods are most effective on a hot, dry day.

Remember that they influence any plant they come into contact with, including weeds and your favorite veggies and perennials, so use them wisely.

Corn gluten

Corn gluten is a byproduct of the maize milling process. It acts as a pre-emergent herbicide, preventing weed seeds from forming roots after germination. To be successful, corn gluten must be applied precisely when a weed germinates.

Flame weeders

For some gardeners, a flame weeder may be the best weed killer. A flame weeder is a propane-fueled torch that burns weed leaves at tremendous temperatures (up to 2,000 degrees Fahrenheit or 1,100 degrees Celsius).

This process, like other non-herbicide methods, must be repeated because the weed's root is sometimes not eliminated even after the leaves are burned. It is most effective against weeds that grow between sidewalk cracks and in gravel.

Flame weeders should never be used around children or pets, near houses or other structures, or during droughts. Flame weeders are illegal in some areas; before purchasing, be sure they are permitted.

In honor of Ralph Waldo Emerson, a truly virtuous weed

Even while it may seem impossible to believe that weeds provide any benefits, they do. They provide habitat and food sources for numerous creatures, as well as adding biodiversity to ecosystems.

Flowers bloom in wilderness regions, providing nectar and pollen for pollinators, seeds for birds, and food for herbivores. Weeds help to avoid soil erosion. When they die and decompose, they contribute organic material to the soil, allowing it to remain healthy and fertile.

Let's look at a common weed, the dandelion

According to the Mount Sinai Health System, dandelions are more nutritious than spinach or kale. They are nutritionally rich in vitamins A, B, C, and D, as well as calcium, iron, potassium, and zinc.

Every part of the dandelion can be consumed. Harvest the leaves while they are young and fragile, before the plant blossoms.

They can be used fresh in salads and sandwiches, sautéed with onions in olive oil, or dried to make tea. The roots can be used to create a coffee-like beverage.

Flowers can be dipped in tempura batter and fried in oil, or they can be made into syrup and jelly.

Traditionally, indigenous peoples of North America used dandelion tea to heal stomach problems, appendicitis, breast irritation, and insufficient milk supply in new mothers.

Insects in your garden

Insects inflict more than $70 billion in annual damage worldwide, destroying 20% to 32% of crops before and after harvest (Bradshaw et al., 2016).

Even if those figures are startling, it is even more shocking to consider that only 1% to 3% of the over one million known insect species are responsible for this devastation.

Most insects are not pests; they are useful and necessary for environmental sustainability. Insects in your garden can cause extensive damage in a short period of time, but there are ways to limit the damage and safeguard plants without using environmentally harmful items.

Another option to help your garden is to employ companion planting, which can repel pests while also attracting beneficial insects.

Understanding your insect rivals

Aphids

Aphids are commonly seen on the undersides of damaged plants' leaves.

Aphids suck the juices from the leaves, which turn yellow, curl, or twist. You may also see a sticky liquid called honeydew on the leaves and beneath the affected plant.

Aphids affect a variety of plants but are particularly drawn to new growth on asparagus, cabbage, cucumbers, eggplant, kale, lettuce, mustard, peppers, potatoes, spinach, tomatoes, and watermelon.

Plant basil, catnip, chives, cilantro, dill, garlic, hyssop, leeks, mint, and nasturtiums to repel aphids.

Cabbage worms

Cabbage worms are the larvae of the white cabbage butterfly. When infestations are severe, entire plants may be defoliated.

Their preferred diet consists of Brassica family vegetables like as cabbage, broccoli, Brussels sprouts, cauliflower, kale, kohlrabi, radishes, and turnips.

Borage, peppermint, tansy, and thyme are all effective repellents for cabbageworms.

Colorado potato beetles

Colorado potato beetles are most active in the spring, and damage (holes in the leaves) is usually visible near the top of the plant.

They are typically seen on eggplant, potato, pepper, tomato, and tomatillo plants.

Catnip, cilantro, onions, and tansy all repel Colorado potato beetles.

Cutworms

Cutworms are big caterpillars that live just below the soil's surface.

If you notice seedlings wilting or severed just above the earth while visiting your garden in the morning, you most certainly have cutworms.

They will attack any seedling, but prefer asparagus, beans, broccoli, cabbage, carrots, celery, corn, kale, lettuce, peas, peppers, potatoes, and tomatoes.

Sage, tansy, and thyme are all effective at repelling cutworms.

Flea beetles

Flea beetles are little leaping insects with lengthy hindlegs.

They emerge from leaf litter in the spring to feed on young plants, causing little round or irregular holes in the leaves of broccoli, cabbage, cauliflower, corn, eggplant, kale, turnips, melons, potatoes, radish, spinach, squash, and tomatoes.

Catnip, hyssop, mint, sage, and thyme are all known to repel flea beetles.

Leaf miner

Leaf miner is a generic term for the larval stage of various insect species, including sawflies and flies.

They tunnel through layers of a leaf's tissue, consuming green cells and creating a visible trail on the leaf's surface.

Depending on the bug type, a wide range of plants can be impacted, including beans, beets, blueberries, cucumber, celery, eggplant, lettuce, nasturtiums, onion, peas, pepper, spinach, squash, Swiss chard, tomato, and watermelon.

Mexican bean beetle

If your bean plants are reduced to skeletonized leaves (just the stem and ribs remain), you have a Mexican bean beetle infestation.

These beetles spend the winter in leaf litter and deposit bright yellow eggs on the undersides of the leaves.

Fennel, garlic, marigolds, potatoes, and rosemary have been shown to repel Mexican bean beetles.

Slugs and snails

Slugs and snails are gastropods, not insects, but they are definitely pests.

Hyssop, marigolds, and rosemary are all effective at repelling slugs and snails.

Spider mites

One of the earliest indicators of a spider mite infestation is a white web on and between the leaves and stems.

Spider mites are extremely minute and impossible to spot without a magnifying glass.

Damage shows first as little brown dots on the leaves, but if the infestation continues, the afflicted leaves will turn yellow. A powerful spray of water from a hose will dislodge the insects.

Basil, broccoli, chives, chrysanthemum, dill, garlic, onions, radishes, rhubarb, and turnips are all effective at repelling spider mites.

Squash bug

Wilted, yellow, dry, and brown leaves are signs of a squash bug infestation.

Cucumbers, melons, pumpkins, squash, and zucchini are all susceptible to squash bug infestation.

Bee balm, catnip, dill, lemon balm, marigolds, radishes, and tansy are all effective squash bug repellents.

Tomato hornworms

Tomato hornworms, as previously said, are typically found on tomatoes and other members of the nightshade or Solanaceae plant family, such as eggplants, peppers and potatoes.

They are enormous green caterpillars (up to 4 inches or 10 centimeters) with white V-shaped stripes and a hook at the back.

Basil, borage, chamomile, dill, and marigolds are all effective at repelling tomato hornworms.

Understanding your insect friends

Several beneficial insects play critical functions in the garden, and understanding what they can do and how they benefit your garden is an important step.

Pollinators

Pollinators include moths, flies, hoverflies, wasps, and beetles, in addition to bees and butterflies. More than 80% of the plants in your garden require pollinators to produce seeds or fruit (Randall, 2020).

Bees

Bees feed on nectar from the flowers they visit. As they fly from one plant to another, pollen accumulates on their bodies and is eventually brushed or groomed into sacs on their legs.

When they return to their nest or hive, they provide pollen to their larvae (offspring).

Bees collect pollen for their own reasons, but they also transport pollen from a flower's male parts (the anthers) to its female parts (the stigmas). This procedure fertilizes the flower's ovaries, causing seeds or fruit to grow.

Bees are drawn to a wide range of flowers, but particularly white, yellow, blue, and purple. They, like many other insects, are unable to see the color red.

Plant basil, cucumber, dill, mint, oregano, peas, rosemary, and other beautiful flowering plants to attract bees to your yard.

Butterflies

Butterflies can travel enormous distances in search of nectar. They favor round flowers with flat petals and tubular nectaries (nectar-producing glands).

Butterflies consume nectar with their long tongues, which function as straws. As they crawl over the flower, pollen gathers on their legs and is transmitted to the next blossom, fertilizing it.

Butterflies enjoy flowers that are yellow, white, pink, red, purple, or pale blue.

Grow fennel, lavender, marjoram, parsley, and other beautiful plants to attract butterflies to your yard.

Moths

Nocturnal moths and diurnal butterflies have many characteristics, yet they are not identical. Moths are better at pollinating flowers than butterflies.

Their fuzzy bodies collect more pollen than butterflies' sleek bodies. Moths visit a wider range of flowers than bees or butterflies (Kaur, 2020).

Moths favor pale colors that are visible at night, such as white, pale yellow, pink, and lavender.

They are also drawn to night-blooming plants that emit intense, pleasant fragrances.

Flies

No, flies are not often seen as beneficial insects, but some species are attracted to sweet-scented flowers and are responsible for pollinating a variety of plants. A recent study found that bees visited 98 out of 105 distinct crops. Flies visited 76.

Furthermore, the flies visited the crops when the weather was cool and there were few bees (Rader et al., 2020). Without the flies, the crops may not have pollinated at lower temperatures.

We wouldn't have chocolate if it weren't for one tiny fly species. The Ceratopogonidae fly is the only insect capable of pollinating cocoa flowers.

Hoverflies

Hoverflies, with their smaller size and bodies, do not collect as much pollen as bees, but they do visit a wide range of plants, particularly those with yellow and white blooms.

Hoverflies only lay eggs on aphid-infested plants; the more aphids present, the more eggs are laid. In addition to aphids, hoverflies consume caterpillars, mealybugs, scales, and thrips.

Planting dill, lemon balm, marigolds, mint, parsley, sweet alyssum, and other decorative blooming plants will attract hoverflies to your yard.

Beetles

Ground beetles are also predators; their capacity to pollinate is innate and occurs while they crawl over flowers in quest of prey.

Beetles are among the oldest insects and pollinators, stretching back over 200 million years. They continue to pollinate plants from the Mesozoic period, such as magnolia, laurels, barberry, and spicebush.

Ground beetles consume caterpillars, cutworms, maggots, snails, and squash bugs.

Moisture under flagstone paving, potted plants, and decaying wood can all bring ground beetles to the garden.

Garden predators

Assassin bugs

Assassin bugs consume aphids, caterpillars, cucumber beetles, tomato hornworms, leafhoppers, and potato beetles.

Plant coriander, dill, and fennel in the garden to attract assassin bugs.

Lacewings

Lacewings consume aphids, mealybugs, mites, thrips, and whiteflies.

Grow coriander, dill, fennel, sunflowers, and tansy in your garden to attract lacewings.

Ladybugs

Ladybugs consume aphids, caterpillars, mealybugs, scale, spider mites, and thrips.

Ladybugs can be drawn to the garden by growing dill, fennel, lemon balm, mint, parsley, and other decorative plants.

Praying mantis

Aphids, bees, beetles, caterpillars, crickets, flies, grasshoppers, leafhoppers, locusts, moths, and spiders are among the insects that praying mantises consume.

Plant dill, fennel, marigolds, and other flowering ornamental plants to attract praying mantises to your garden.

Robber flies

Robber flies consume bees, beetles, dragonflies, grasshoppers, leafhoppers, spiders, and wasps.

Grow catnip, chamomile, and mint in your garden to attract robber flies.

Spiders

Spiders devour aphids, bees, flies, grasshoppers, and wasps.

Spiders can be attracted to the garden by ground covers, rocky nooks, wood heaps, and disturbed areas.

Parasitoid insects

Some insects (known as parasitoids) deposit eggs on or inside the bodies of insect pests (hosts). The eggs hatch, and the larvae begin to feed on the pest, eventually killing it.

Parasitic wasps

Parasitoid wasps (Hymenoptera, Brachonid, and Trichogramma) are far smaller than those found on the picnic table. Adults eat on nectar and pollen.

They don't make nests or sting like other wasps. They lay their eggs inside an egg or caterpillar, which is consumed once the larval wasp emerges.

Planting allium, cilantro, dill, fennel, and other decorative plants will attract parasitic wasps to your garden.

Tachinid flies

Tachinid flies have a similar appearance to houseflies. Adults feed on flowers nectar and the sticky excrement (honeydew) of aphids and scale insects. Some species lay their eggs on plant material that is consumed by the pest. The pest's eggs hatch inside its body.

Other species place their eggs on the pest's body. When the larvae hatch, they burrow into the host. The larvae begin feeding on the pest from the inside.

Planting cilantro, dill, fennel, parsley, chamomile, and other beautiful blooming plants will attract tachinid flies to your yard.

Pest control methods for your garden

Acceptable tolerance

Insects are a natural part of gardening, and you will never be able to entirely eliminate them (nor would you want to). A healthy, biodiverse habitat must be inhabited by a variety of creatures.

Pests hurt your plants, but they also provide food for birds and other creatures. When remediation is essential, utilize the least harmful means to control the damage and restore it to an acceptable level.

Maintaining garden health through proper maintenance

The first step in pest management is to maintain your gardens health, which begins with the soil. Healthy soil produces healthy plants, which are better equipped to withstand pests and illnesses.

The diversity of organisms in good soil is greater than in poor soil. A diversified population increases competition, limiting the potential of soil-borne pests and illnesses to spread unchecked.

Trophobiosis

Francis Chaboussou (who died in 1985) created the hypothesis of trophobiosis. He was a plant researcher who worked at France's Institute National de la Recherche Agronomique (INRA). The hypothesis proposes that healthy plants growing in healthy soil are 'understandable' to insect pests.

Chaboussou argued that chemical pesticides harmed plants, making them weaker, more attractive to pests, and subject to attack. This idea explains, on a molecular level, why pesticides lose efficiency with time, forcing farmers to employ higher doses or more frequent applications.

The prevailing thinking is that insects acquire resistance to pesticides over time. Chaboussou disagreed, arguing that the more pesticides used, the weaker the plant becomes and the more attractive it becomes to pests, resulting in a cycle of greater pesticide use (Chaboussou, 1985).

Other factors

Appropriate water management fosters a healthy garden. Plants that are over-, under-, or inconsistently watered are less able to withstand pests.

Choosing plants and plant kinds that are appropriate for the climate and growing season aids in the maintenance of a healthy garden.

Diseases are prevented from spreading between plants by quickly removing diseased plants and contaminated organic debris from the garden, as well as cleaning gardening tools.

Mindfulness

Please be aware of the garden's daily changes as you spend time there throughout the season. Watch your plants grow from tiny seedlings to healthy plants that blossom and produce fruit. Take note of the colors of the leaves as they grow.

Observing them will help you get to know them, and you'll quickly start to spot minor changes that could be early warning signs of difficulties. There are numerous pest-monitoring methods available.

Look for signs of damage such as holes, wilting, yellowing, webbing, sticky or powdery substances, excrement on leaves and stems, and missing plants.

Place a wide sheet of white paper beneath the plant and gently tap it; insects will be expelled and fall onto the paper. Try to identify any pests you see; knowing the type and amount of pests will help you plan your approach to control.

Many insects are active at night; some are tiny and difficult to spot, while others hide on the underside of leaves.

If you can't see the pest to identify it, take note of which plants are damaged; many insect pests are plant-specific. The type of plant, the sight of the damage, and an online search can all help narrow down the identification.

Garden control methods: Monitoring, exclusion, repellent, and removal

In organic gardening, the goal is to constantly utilize the least offensive method possible to control the problem.

Row covers

Row covers offer plants with sunlight, water, and air while also protecting them from insects. Made of woven cloth, they are typically hung on top of the plants or over hoops above the garden during planting, when young plants are most vulnerable.

Because this is an exclusion method of control, the covers must be securely fastened so that there are no access spots.

If the bed has previously been infested with soil-borne pests (flea beetles, onion, or corn maggots), do not place a row cover over it unless a separate, unrelated, or unsusceptible crop is grown.

Row covers can be left in place all season if pollination is not required. Plants that require insect pollination must have their coverings removed once they begin to flower.

Yellow sticky traps

Place sticky traps throughout your garden. The increased quantity of insects in the trap will show the severity of the infestation. You'll be able to detect whether pest activity is getting worse.

Pay great attention to the many sorts of insects in the trap. Sticky traps make no distinction between pests and beneficial insects. If you notice a large quantity of beneficial insects, remove the traps as soon as possible.

Pheromone traps

Pheromones are scent molecules produced by insects. Pheromone traps use a sex pheromone or an aggregation (gathering) pheromone to attract insects to a collection bottle.

They can be used to monitor pest populations or eradicate them from the environment. These traps are species-specific, so they will not work for all insects. Because they work by attracting pests, they must be kept away from the garden.

When working with insect attractants, always use disposable gloves.

Crop rotation

Crop rotation is an effective approach to keeping soil healthy. It also serves as an effective insect management technique.

Many pests spend some of their lives or overwinter in the soil. At the end of their lives, the adults would lay their eggs in the soil near where the plants they ate were growing.

When the eggs hatch or the adults emerge in the following season, they will seek out their favored plant. If crops have been rotated, that plant will be unavailable to them.

Trap crops

Some plants attract more bug pests than others. You can utilize this feature to defend your vegetables by strategically planting traps or sacrificial crops near (but not in) your garden.

Trap crops and the pests they attract

- Amaranth: Cucumber. Beetle
- Calendula: Slug.
- Chervil: Slug, Snail.
- Collard: Cabbage Worm.
- Dill: Tomato Hornworm
- Eggplant: Colorado potato beetle
- Marigold: Root Nematode.
- Millet: Squash Bug
- Mustard: Tarnish bug
- Nasturtium: Aphid, flea beetle
- Okra: Aphid

- Parsley: Slug, snail

- Radish: Flea beetle

- Sorghum: Corn earworm

- Sunflower: Stink bug

- Tansy: Colorado potato beetle

- Zinnia: Japanese beetle

When the trap plant becomes contaminated, pick it up, wash it in a bucket of soapy water to kill the pests, and discard it in your compost bin. You can plant trap crops in succession to ensure continuous protection throughout the growing season.

Growing vertically

Training vines up trellises protects vining plants like squash and tomatoes by keeping fruit and stems off the ground and away from crawling pests.

Water spray

A powerful spray of water from a hose can remove many smaller, soft-bodied pests, such as aphids, from plants. The spray inflicts enough damage on the insects that they are unable to climb back onto the plant.

Hand picking

Larger insects can be controlled by handpicking them off the plant and immersing them in a bucket of water containing a few drops of dish soap. If you see tomato hornworms or other caterpillars with "rice" on their bodies, leave them in the garden.

The rice-like attachments are parasitoid wasp cocoons that, once hatched and matured, will help safeguard your plants.

Pruning infested plants

During the early stages of an infestation, you may see one or two branches of a plant with clusters of insects or eggs. Prune the affected sections of the plant and soak the branches in soapy water before composting them.

Collars

Collars around the stems of tomatoes, squash, and other plants can help protect them against cutworms and squash borers.

Collars can be manufactured from various materials, including paper towel rolls, aluminum foil, milk cartons, plastic drinking cups, and yogurt containers.

Even bamboo skewers wrapped around stems can keep cutworms from girdling the plant. Collars should be pressed into the soil to keep pests from burrowing underneath.

Copper strips can be placed around plants or pots; slugs and snails will not cross over them.

Biological pest control

Biological pest management methods include the use of living organisms such as predators and parasitoids, as well as pathogens. Insects, like humans and animals, can become infected with disease-causing germs.

Bacillus thuringiensis, also known as Bt, is a naturally occurring soil-borne bacteria that can target and kill specific insect species while remaining safe to others. Nematodes are another example of soil pathogens that infect insects.

Both diseases can be sprayed on soil or plants and are safe for humans, animals, birds, plants, and non-targeted insects.

Neem oil

Neem oil is a natural insecticide derived from the seeds of a tropical tree. It can be applied to insect pests or used as a preventative.

It will harm beneficial insects, so use it carefully early in the day before they are active.

Diatomaceous earth

Diatomaceous earth is a powder derived from fossilized plant debris. Slugs, snails, and crawling insects can be effectively controlled. Unfortunately, it is not specific and can harm beneficial insects.

Avoid using it near flowers. When purchasing diatomaceous earth, search for food-grade materials that are safe to use around children and pets.

Homemade insecticide recipes:

A word of caution before spraying anything in your garden.

1. Test them on a few leaves before spraying the entire plant.

2. Mark the bottles with a waterproof marker.

3. Shake the mixes before and during use to ensure that the solutions are thoroughly distributed.

4. To avoid leaf burn, spray the leaves away from direct sunlight.

5. If there are beneficial insects present, do not spray the plants.

Insecticide soap spray

Commercial insecticidal soap is available at large box retailers and garden centers, but it is simple to produce yourself. It effectively controls aphids, mites, and mealybugs. The soap mixture removes a protective covering from the insects' skin.

- One gallon of distilled water.

- 2 1/2 teaspoons (38 mL) of mild liquid soap

- 2 1/2 tablespoons (38 mL) of vegetable oil

Add the soap and oil to the distilled water and carefully combine. Pour the contents into two spray bottles and label them with a waterproof marker. Apply as needed to afflicted plants.

Vegetable oil spray

Aphids, mites, and thrips can be controlled with a vegetable oil spray. It acts by covering the insects' body and keeping them from breathing.

- 1 cup (237 mL) of vegetable oil
- 1 tablespoon (15 mL) dish soap
- 1 quart (.95 liter) of distilled water in a spray bottle.

Combine the vegetable oil and dish soap in a jar. Pour 2 teaspoons (10 mL) of the oil-soap combination into the spray container. Shake the mixture carefully before spraying it on the afflicted plants.

Garlic spray

Garlic spray is effective against aphids, mites, caterpillars, armyworms, cutworms, beetles, slugs, mosquitos, and flies. It will kill soft-bodied pests when directly sprayed, although it is primarily employed as a repellant.

Garlic has a strong odor that repels many pests. To avoid deterring pollinators, do not spray it directly on the flowers.

Garlic is harmful to rabbits, dogs, and cats.

- 2 whole garlic cloves.
- 1 teaspoon (5 mL) dish soap.
- 1/2 cup (119 mL) of vegetable oil

- 1 quart (.95 liters) of distilled water in a spray bottle.

In a blender, combine the garlic cloves with a tiny amount of water. Let the mixture sit for about 12 hours before straining it into a jar.

Add the dish soap and vegetable oil, then fill the jar with water. In a spray bottle, combine 1 cup (237 mL) of the garlic combination and 1 quart (.95 liters) of water.

Shake the mixture vigorously and spray the afflicted plants.

Tomato leaf spray

Tomato leaf spray is effective against aphids and spider mites. Tomato leaves contain an organic alkaloid substance that is poisonous to insects.

- 2 cups (500 mL) of chopped tomato leaves (choose fresh leaves from the base of the plants)
- 1 quart (.95 liter) of hot water
- Use a few drops of dish soap.

Pour the heated water over the tomato leaves and leave them to steep overnight.

Strain the liquid into a spray bottle.

Add the dish soap and shake it well to combine the ingredients.

Conclusion

When it comes to weed and pest control, it can feel like you've been picking weeds all day. At the same time, you feel as if you have abandoned your vegetables to pluck weeds.

Using the information provided in this chapter, you can determine which vegetables belong and which do not. Pest control is another important skill that many inexperienced gardeners ignore.

That being said, knowledge gained through observations, applications, and a deep respect for nature's rhythms benefits the soil, plants, and gardeners alike.

The methods you've learned here will serve you well, season after season, for years to come.

Chapter 9

How to Harvest, Store, and Winterize an Organic Garden.

When it comes to harvesting any garden, there are a few important elements to consider. First, confirm that the plants are ripe and ready for harvesting.

This can be determined by looking up the maturity date for the individual type of plant being grown or by just inspecting the plant to see if it has achieved the appropriate size and color.

Harvest timing is also an essential aspect. Some plants are best picked in the morning when temperatures are lower, while others are best harvested in the afternoon when the sun is at its highest.

It is also critical to harvest the plants at the appropriate time of year, when the weather conditions are ideal for growth and development.

Correct harvesting practices might help you maximize your garden's produce. This includes harvesting the plants with sharp tools, keeping them cool and dry, and properly cleaning them before consumption.

Harvesting for optimum yield

With their delicate textures and transient freshness, leafy greens necessitate a light touch and prompt intervention.

Harvesting is best done in the morning, when the garden still has the chill of the night.

Greens, nestled in the dew's embrace, preserve their sharpness, which lessens as the day warms.

Using a sharp knife or scissors, make a clean cut at the base of the stem to leave the plant's roots intact, potentially stimulating second growth.

Root vegetables, which are hidden gems in the soil's depth, announce their readiness to the surface.

A diligent excavation with hands diving into the earth reveals mature roots of all sizes and colors peeping through the dirt.

Gentle tugging, assisted by loosening the surrounding dirt, releases these buried treasures with minimal damage, keeping their purity and taste.

Successive harvesting to extend the growing season

The concept of successive harvesting, similar to staggered start times in a relay race, assures a consistent crop that expands the season's offerings.

This approach entails periodically harvesting mature plants to make way for the growth of those that have been sown or planted at regular intervals.

For example, removing mature lettuce leaves allows younger plants to grow and thrive, transforming a single planting into a renewable source of greens.

Similarly, picking root vegetables such as beets and carrots at different stages of maturity ensures a consistent supply, avoiding the all-at-once abundance that frequently leads to waste.

How to harvest flowers

Flowers combine beauty and utility. Their pollen-filled blossoms bring joy. Harvesting flowers, whether for a vase or a pollinator, takes a keen eye for timing; early morning, once again, is ideal, capturing the blossoms at their most brilliant.

A diagonal cut along the stem, just above a node or leaf junction, promotes further development and possible reblooming.

For plants intended for indoor display, fast immersion in water prolongs their freshness, bringing the garden's charm into the home.

Make harvesting easier and more efficient

Harvest efficiency is more than just saving time; it is also about preserving the garden's vitality for future yields.

Carefully selected and maintained tools are critical; ergonomic designs decrease strain, while sharp blades enable clean cuts that heal rapidly, thus preventing disease.

A systematic technique, moving gradually across the beds, guarantees that each plant is noticed.

Containers placed within easy reach reduce unneeded back and forth, keeping the focus on the task at hand.

Sharing harvesting knowledge with the next generation

Involving children in the harvest transforms the garden into a classroom, teaching lessons about nature's cycles in the rows. Picking berries or cherry tomatoes provides quick benefits and is simple enough for young hands.

Explaining the signals of ripeness, the feel of a ready tomato, or the color of a perfect berry fosters an appreciation for both the fruit and the process.

This involvement not only provides aid, but it also plants seeds of knowledge and appreciation for the natural environment, growing the future generation of gardeners.

Harvest activities for children that are fun and educational

Berry picking: Take the children to the garden and let them join in the fun of picking berries. Show children how to identify ripe berries and let them feel the excitement of discovering and gathering them. You may also use this as an opportunity to teach children about the plant's lifecycle and the importance of harvesting at the appropriate time.

Cherry tomato quest: Lead the children on a rewarding treasure hunt to find and gather cherry tomatoes. Give them baskets and let them roam the garden, looking for the ripest and juiciest tomatoes. This pastime is not only enjoyable, but it also teaches kids the value of plant care and the sweet benefits of their efforts.

Harvesting basket: Give each child their own basket and let them help with the harvest by gathering ripe produce from the garden. Offer to compete and see who can fill their basket first. This is a great opportunity for kids to learn about different plant varieties and growth stages, making it both entertaining and instructive.

Carrot creatures: Encourage children to pick and clean carrots. Add toothpicks and glue, as well as other garden vegetable pieces. They can use their imagination and ingenuity to develop their own distinct characters and stories, using carrots as a foundation. It's a pleasant and nutritious method to get kids to eat vegetables while having fun.

Clean, prepare, and store vegetables, herbs, and flowers

The journey from garden to storage begins with a cleansing ritual, which removes the earth's leftovers and any remaining guests. When cleaning veggies, use soft and sparing water to remove the soil from the outside.

For root vegetables, use a soft brush to break up any obstinate clumps without injuring the delicate skin that protects the flesh from deterioration.

Herbs and flowers, on the other hand, require a gentler touch, a rinsing that whispers rather than roars, in order to preserve their ethereal beauty and delicate structures.

This initial cleaning, followed by meticulous drying, prepares each item for the journey ahead, ensuring that moisture, the harbinger of mildew and rot, does not follow them into storage.

Ideal storage conditions for a wide range of produce

Learn about the storage requirements for fruits, vegetables, and herbs. Root vegetables, for example, like cool and gloomy conditions, such as a basement or a storage bin packed with moist sand; which resembles the soil from which they were collected, keeping them fresh.

Leafy greens, on the other hand, prefer the humidity and crispness of the crisper drawer in the refrigerator, where they are wrapped to prevent wilting. Herbs have a great aroma and should be stored in an open area with good ventilation and warmth.

Bundle them with twine or string and hang upside down. Flowers can be cut and kept in a vase filled with water, creating a temporary garden as they unfold.

Processing options for your harvest

The harvest's abundance frequently exceeds the immediate capacity for consumption, spurring a shift toward preservation methods that capture the essence of the season for later enjoyment.

The simplest of these procedures, drying, allows moisture to evaporate, which concentrates flavors and improves shelf life, transforming herbs and select vegetables into pantry mainstays.

Canning, a ballet of heat, acidity, and timing, preserves the garden's harvest in jars, preventing spoilage and providing a taste of summer in the colder months.

Though less common, freeze drying is a modern alchemy that sublimates moisture while preserving structure and nutrition, resulting in lightweight, long-lasting products.

Choose a method according to your available time and technology, taking into account the probability of future food scarcity.

Harvesting your garden can rekindle your love of cooking

I enjoy cooking, especially with freshly grown fruits and vegetables. It is a fantastic way to bring people together while preparing delicious food.

Unfortunately, many people nowadays are disconnected from the work of growing and gathering their own food.

This is a shame because producing and cooking your own produce is quite fulfilling. We'll look at how it could rekindle your love of cooking by harvesting your garden.

Growing your own produce provides you with not only fresh and healthy nutrients, but also the opportunity to experiment with new flavors and sensations. If you cultivate your own tomatoes, you can prepare fresh tomato sauce for your pasta or a tasty salsa.

If you have an herb garden, you can utilize fresh herbs to enhance the flavor and complexity of your cuisine. There is no limit to what you can accomplish with your own produce!

One of the benefits of harvesting your organic garden is that it inspires you to be creative. When you have an abundance of a specific vegetable, you may need to find creative ways to use it. This can result in some quite delicious and imaginative foods.

For example, if you have a lot of zucchini, consider making zucchini fritters or zucchini bread. If you have a lot of plants, you can prepare herb-infused oils and vinegars.

Harvesting your garden helps you to be more environmentally mindful. Growing your own produce allows you to know exactly where it came from and how it was grown. This means you can avoid the toxic pesticides and other chemicals commonly used in commercial agriculture.

Furthermore, by growing your own food, you reduce the amount of transportation required to bring your food from farm to table.

Drying and preserving herbs and edible flowers

Drying and preserving herbs and edible flowers is an excellent skill that requires patience and technique. It is significant because it allows us to savor the essence of summer's riches year round.

Different ways might be utilized, but they all have the same purpose: to help us connect with the botanical riches that flourish in our gardens.

Drying and storing these gems allows us to extend their lives beyond the seasons. This process occurs as the garden prepares for the upcoming winter.

Air drying

Herbal preservation is a time-honored practice. First, take tiny bunches of herbs and tie them to the stems with a simple knot that binds but does not restrict.

These bunches are hung upside down in a warm, dry, well-ventilated area away from direct sunlight. Over time, the herbs gradually lose moisture, resulting in a dried form that retains their flavor and medicinal characteristics.

This technique protects the delicate structures of herbs and prepares them for usage in times of scarcity.

Oven drying

For those wanting a faster road to preservation, the oven provides a modern hearth where heat and airflow combine in the drying process. The meticulously detailed preparation includes a cleansing to preserve integrity, followed by a patting dry to anticipate the oven's embrace.

The herbs and flowers rest on trays, their forms a testament to the garden's diversity. Preheat the oven to the lowest setting. Close monitoring and a keen eye are required to ensure that the essence of the herbs is kept while avoiding the harshness of excessive heat.

A combination of temperature and time helps dried plants preserve their color, aroma, and flavor.

Dehydrator drying

The dehydrator is intended to dry herbs and edible flowers at low temperature. It works by distributing warm air evenly over each leaf and petal.

The process begins with gently washing the botanicals, which are then carefully arranged on the dehydrator trays, taking into account the space required for each.

The dehydrator is designed to manage the botanicals' sensitive nature, ensuring that the dried items preserve their essence and structure while being suitable for storage.

Storage

The final step in the preservation of herbs and edible flowers is storage. This consideration is critical for preserving the vitality captured during drying.

Glass jars are a perfect vessel because of their transparency, which allows you to see the colors and textures within. They also have a seal that keeps moisture and light out.

Labeling these containers becomes an exercise in order and anticipation, with each name promising future flavors and solutions.

The dried herbs and flowers, with their jars decorated with ribbons and tags, provide an option for gift-giving for people who are creative.

This personal touch elevates the harvest to an act of sharing. This sharing, an extension of the gardens' generosity, bridges the gap between person and community, A concrete expression of the cycle of development, preservation, and regeneration.

In this peaceful part of the garden's cycle, when the buzz of bees and the fragrance of blooms have given way to the quietness of preservation, the gardener's thoughtfulness is demonstrated by drying and storing herbs and edible flowers.

Each approach, chosen for its fit to the task and household routines, represents a profound connection to the earth's produce and a dedication to honoring and expanding its wealth.

This participation is more than just a duty; it is a celebration of the garden's blessings, honoring the bounty that nourishes us and planning for future cycles.

Preparing for winter

As fall goes by, the garden's palette becomes more muted, with colors of amber and russet. This seasonal transition represents a decrease in the garden's outward productivity and the start of a period of preparation and protection.

The steps taken during these cooler months are critical to ensuring that the garden beds can endure the winter chill and emerge in the spring, ready to sustain an entirely fresh, and new growth cycle.

Cleaning up spent plants and debris

The first task is to clear the season's residue. Spent plants have completed their life cycles, and debris, the leftovers of a season's growth, must be carefully removed from the beds.

This cleansing, rather than simply tidying, serves several purposes. It eliminates potential breeding grounds for pests and diseases—organisms that could overwinter in the stubble and jeopardize the following season's crops.

Furthermore, this activity allows the soil to be exposed to air and sunshine, both of which are necessary for soil rejuvenation.

The deliberate removal of this organic matter, while leaving any healthy root systems to degrade naturally, preserves the garden bed's intricate web of life, including the microbial and insect communities that support its fertility.

Protecting the soil with mulch and organic matter

Once removed, the garden beds benefit from being layered with mulch and organic materials, which serves as both a blanket and a banquet for the soil.

Mulch insulates the soil in a variety of ways, from straw and leaf mold to wood chips, reducing temperature variations that might disrupt the microbial life necessary for soil health.

This cover also reduces evaporation, allowing the soil to retain its moisture balance even when the garden is not in use.

Beyond protection, integrating organic matter, such as compost or well-rotted manure, improves the soil and replenishes nutrients lost during the growth season.

This enrichment does not provide immediate gratification but rather a gradual infusion of life as the organic matter degrades throughout the winter, weaving its essence into the soil's structure.

This technique, a marriage of protection and sustenance, guarantees that the garden beds awaken in the spring, brimming with life and ready to support the new planting season.

The benefits of planting cover crops

In the solitude of garden beds ready for winter's dormancy, sowing cover crops emerges as a foresight act, a living investment in the garden's future growth. These crops, chosen for their capacity to survive in the cooler months, serve numerous purposes.

They mitigate soil erosion by having their roots stabilize the soil against winter's scouring winds and rains. They inhibit weeds by out-competing them for space and light.

Perhaps most importantly, they enrich the soil; legumes, for example, transform nitrogen from the air into a form that may be used by future plants.

The process for sowing these helpful guardians into prepared beds is simple, but effective. Seeds distributed by hand over the soil's surface require only a light covering of earth to ensure their promise, which is fulfilled in the spring when the cover crops are chopped down and converted into the soil.

This inclusion symbolizes the end of their cycle, with their bodies breaking down to release the nutrients they have gathered--a legacy that will support the following season's growth.

During the garden's quieter months, the beds serve as containers of potential for the upcoming season rather than monuments to the past.

The tasks conducted when winter approaches, such as cleaning spent plants and debris, replenishing the soil with mulch and organic matter, and establishing cover crops, are rituals rather than chores.

They are acknowledgements of the garden's cyclical nature, gestures of care that honor past productivity while preparing for future rebirth.

Following these simple steps transforms the garden beds from growth containers into loving habitats that encourage regeneration, demonstrating the gardener's care and the earth's natural fertility as it prepares for spring planting.

Winterization of perennial plants

As the garden winds down for the winter, gardeners concentrate on caring for the remaining plants. These plants contributed significantly to the garden's beauty and aroma over the summer, and they are now in a state of transition, preparing for the following season.

During this time, gardeners quietly care for the plants, conserving and preserving them while preparing them for the next cycle of growth.

Soil care and improvement

Perennial plants require a rich soil to grow healthy and strong. During the winter, the garden soil need attention to provide the plants with the nutrients they require.

Organic ingredients such as compost, bone meal, and kelp are carefully mixed into the soil to improve it. These components are combined and worked into the top layer of soil.

Over the winter, they decompose and provide a rich humus. In the spring, this humus will replenish the soil with nutrients, ensuring that the plants have everything they require to thrive.

Garden bed care in preparation for winter

As the cold weather rolls in, that lovely garden bed needs to be prepared as well. Perennial plants require recuperation following their growing season.

During this time, they rely on the soil for warmth and moisture, which is made possible by the way the garden bed is laid out.

If you have a raised garden bed, ensure that a good drainage system is in place to prevent root rot caused by excess water.

It is also vital to evaluate the garden bed for signs of wear and tear (which happen) and repair any damage before the snow and freezing temperatures cause further damage.

By completing these simple things, the garden bed will be strengthened and prepared for winter.

Perennial herbs and flowers can survive the winter

Each perennial herb and flower has distinct needs that necessitate a tailored approach to overwintering.

For example, lavender and sage, which have Mediterranean origins, require a dry, chilly environment and benefit from a gravel border that deflects excess precipitation.

On the other hand, more fragile plants like chives and parsley, tucked among the garden's greenery, may enjoy warmth behind a cover shield without being suffocated.

This care, adapted to each species, indicates the gardener's understanding that winter is not a time for neglect, but rather a distinct type of attention that respects the hibernation required for renewal.

Mulching methods used to protect against frost

Mulch, at this point in the gardener's journey, is an effective aid for protecting perennials during the winter. It can be made of various materials, including straw and leaves.

Straw, when placed in a thick layer, can insulate the soil and trap heat while also permitting gas exchange. Meanwhile, collected leaves in the fall can nourish the soil by decomposing and forming a frost barrier.

It is critical to apply the appropriate amount of mulch based on each plant's tolerance to cold and moisture. This will safeguard the plants from unexpected winter weather.

Perennial pruning ensures optimal spring growth

Pruning, the deliberate process of removing something, is viewed as a development of potential rather than a subtraction. Perennials' faded leaves and wasted blossoms are carefully clipped away, leaving only the plant's essential parts ready for spring.

This careful pruning, driven by a thorough understanding of each plant's growth habits, opens the perennial's architecture, allowing air and light to permeate and eliminating moisture, which fosters disease.

It is a preparation that speaks to the future, to the spurts of growth that will signal the return of warmth and life to the garden.

During this peaceful period of preparation, the winter garden becomes a hub of subtle activity, with the gardener's actions laying the basis for the upcoming seasons.

Perennial winterization, a series of operations carried out with care and foresight, is infused with an understanding of the garden's development and dormancy cycles.

This care, a combination of science and art, knowledge and intuition, guarantees that when the garden beds rest beneath their winter mantle, they are ready to rise with vigor as the seasonal cycle turns toward the sun.

Planning for the next season

After the first frost blankets the garden, it remains still, encouraging us to reflect on the year's triumphs and trials while also anticipating the possibilities of future seasons.

The garden's continuous cycle of growth, dormancy, and rebirth provides a sense of closure while moving us forward into future activities in the fertile soil.

Reviewing the previous growth season

A gardener's expertise comes not just from caring for the soil, but also from learning from each season's achievements and disappointments.

Evaluating the year's triumphs and failures is critical to gaining a real understanding of how you performed.

A gardener can make the essential changes and innovations for a healthy organic garden by analyzing trends and irregularities.

Crop rotation, a traditional farming strategy derived from this procedure, allows gardeners to relocate plant families to different parts of the garden.

This strategy feeds the soil, prevents pests and diseases, provides nutrients, and keeps garden beds productive and healthy ecosystems.

Creating a planting plan for next year

Using the previous season's findings, establishing a planting strategy for the following year becomes a creative endeavor anchored in empirical wisdom. This sophisticated yet customizable plan rearranges the garden to reflect lessons learnt from the previous year.

Observations regarding sunlight patterns, water requirements, and companion planting success inform a mosaic of garden beds that promise not only productivity but also harmony.

This technique, while aspirational, is founded in reality—a balance of ambition and demonstrated competence in the garden—ensuring that each seed sown in future seasons offers the promise of progress, learning, and beauty.

Reflections & learning

Gardeners can use the winter to take a vacation from physical effort and focus on personal development. Books provide a wealth of information and inspiration from gardeners all over the world (hint, hint).

Both in-person and online seminars allow you to learn from others and build a sense of community. Gardening groups and forums are an excellent way to network with other gardeners and develop a better understanding of the subject.

Gardeners can provide a solid foundation for future gardening initiatives by utilizing this time to learn and improve.

Holiday decoration ideas for garden beds

During the winter, the garden beds are lifeless, but they can be transformed into a festive scene with modest decorations that express the season's delight.

If you have raised beds, drape them with strings of lights to simulate the garden's brightness in the summer, while wreaths and garlands created from garden produce add to the festive atmosphere.

These decorations serve as a reminder that, even in its slumber, the garden is still a source of life, connection, and hope.

By dressing up its naked bones to commemorate the cycle of life, the garden helps us bridge the gap between the growing season and the end of the year.

As we conclude this chapter, envision the garden waiting for the following season. The garden symbolizes the year's hard work and future growth.

The gardener's trip is similar to the cycle of seasons: planting, growing, harvesting, and relaxing. It's similar to learning, growing, and looking ahead.

To keep the garden alive and evolving, we plan for the next season based on previous experiences and future goals. This ensures that the garden remains a vivid and ever-changing representation of the natural world.

Final thoughts

The garden is an area where we can meaningfully engage with nature. It is a place where we aim for a balance of sustainability, diversity, and aesthetics. To achieve this equilibrium, we use realistic principles based on hardiness zones, succession planting, and seasonal planning.

These methods provide a road map for our trip, guiding us through the complexities of the ecosystem while meeting our goal to develop and care for life. By adhering to these criteria, we can construct an organic garden that supports and nourishes our surroundings.

Chapter 10
Conclusion

Thank you for reading, "Organic Gardening for Beginners." My goal is that you have taken this environmentally conscious gardening strategy to heart and are embarking on the journey to become the protector of your own organic garden.

I hope this book has given you useful insights and resources to improve your gardening experience. By practicing organic gardening, you not only improve the health of your garden but also contribute to a healthier environment. Your efforts to simplify pest management, improve soil quality, and increase yields are critical to building a sustainable and successful garden.

These pages featured numerous practical lessons, such as the origins of organic gardening, the vital importance of soil preparation, growing a naturally healthy garden, making use of your natural resources, the value of composting and recycling, the wisdom of weed and pest control, and how to harvest, store, and winterize your organic garden. These teachings aim to pave the path for a gardening method that is both enriching and sustainable.

Organic gardening is an ongoing process of discovery and growth. Exchanging experiences with others increases the individual gardener's experience while also contributing to a greater culture of support, knowledge exchange, and collaborative learning.

I would like to offer my heartfelt gratitude to all of the gardeners who have decided to garden organically. Your nurturing helps to create a greener and more vibrant world. Gardening is about cultivating plants and leaving a legacy of environmental harmony and connectedness. As this book concludes, another begins, with you as the author, offering new growth, discoveries, and happiness.

Continue to grow and prosper, and remember that gardening is a step toward a better, more sustainable future. I wish you and your garden much success in the adventures that await.

P.S. Please see my Amazon author page for further trips into sustainable living and personal well-being.

Chapter 11
Thank You From the Author

Wow, what an incredible journey we've had together! I sincerely hope you enjoyed it. If you did, please take a few moments to review this book.

Every review is important to me, and I read and consider each one carefully.

Not only does your feedback enable me to continue writing inspiring books, but it is also the primary reason this book is viewed and thus considered by more people who wish to start their own gardening journey.

You help us and them, and together, we help the world. Teamwork!

Thank you for being the best part of this book and for helping to create a community in which we can grow together and find all we need to live our lives to the fullest.

Thank you sincerely.

ORGANIC GARDENING FOR BEGINNERS

G. F. Quinn

Chapter 12
Resources

Google. (n.d.-d). https://www.google.ca/

Wikipedia contributors. (2024a, June 18). *Outline of organic gardening and farming*. Wikipedia. https://en.wikipedia.org/wiki/Outline_of_organic_gardening_and_farming

Adamchak, R. (2024, June 15). *Organic farming | Definition, History, Methods, Practices, & Benefits*. Encyclopedia Britannica. https://www.britannica.com/topic/organic-farming

Sakawsky, A., & Sakawsky, A. (2020, December 30). A complete guide to organic gardening for beginners, The House & Homestead. *The House & Homestead - Helping you create, grow, and live a good life... From scratch!* https://thehouseandhomestead.com/organic-gardening-beginners/

Hailey, L. (2023, October 6). *Organic Gardening 101 for Beginners: How to start an organic garden*. Epic Gardening. https://www.epicgardening.com/organic-gardening/

Reid-StJohn, S. (2018, April 2). *Organic gardening for beginners*. Bonnie Plants. https://bonnieplants.com/blogs/garden-fundamentals/organic-gardening-for-beginners

wordpress. (2020, September 19). How to start an organic garden for beginners - EARTH'S ALLY®. *Earth's Ally - Safe for People, Pets & Planet.* https://earthsally.com/gardening-basics/organic-gardening-for-beginners.html

Phil. (2024, February 8). *Organic Vegetable Gardening For Beginners - 7 Tips.* Smiling Gardener. https://www.smilinggardener.com/organic-vegetable-gardening/vegetable-gardening-for-beginners/

Garden Organic | Beginner guide. (2022, November 18). Garden Organic. https://www.gardenorganic.org.uk/expert-advice/beginner-guide

Lombardo, L. (2021). *Organic gardening for beginners: An Eco-Friendly Guide to Growing Vegetables, Fruits, and Herbs.* Rockridge Press.

Quinn, G. F. (2023). *Raised-Bed gardening for beginners: A Complete Guide To Growing A Healthy Organic Garden On A Budget, Using Tools And Materials You Probably Already Have!* Personal Development Publishing.

Chapter 13
Also by G.F. Quinn

Edmonton Made Easy:Super Easy Guide To Discover The Most Popular Local Attractions, Restaurants, Hiking Trails & Activities While Exploring The City of Champions!

Raised-Bed Gardening for Beginners: A Complete Guide To Growing A Healthy Organic Garden On A Budget, Using Tools And Materials You Probably Already Have!

Type 2 Diabetes Cookbook for Beginners: Quick and Easy Mouth-Watering Recipes to Help Manage Type 2 Diabetes: A Better Way to Eat Healthy Without Sacrificing Your Taste Buds!

Traditional Shadow Work for Beginners: A guided spiritual journey through healing for beginners | Using a traditional approach to finding, healing, and integrating your shadow self.

Printed in Great Britain
by Amazon